The Student MONEY GUIDE

Andrew Moore
and
Graham Roberts

The Student
MONEY
GUIDE

Andrew Moore
and
Graham Roberts

CURTIS

Published by William Curtis Limited
83 Clerkenwell Road
London EC1R 5AR

First published 1989

Line illustrations by Chen Ling

Typeset by Area Graphics Ltd, Letchworth

Printed in Great Britain by Richard Clay, Bungay, Suffolk

British Library Cataloguing in Publication Data
Moore, Andrew
    The student money guide.
    1. Personal finance – Manuals
    I. Title
    332.024

    ISBN 1-871967-02-3

To
May Josephine Baker
and
Muriel Benison, MA (Oxon)

The most usual form of financial disagreement between parents and their offspring is caused by non-communication.

ACKNOWLEDGEMENTS

We wish to thank the many individuals
and organisations who have assisted us
during the research and preparation of this book.
It is not possible to mention all by name
but we would particularly wish to express
our gratitude to: Harold Andrew, Adam Gaines,
National Union of Students, Tony Quirk,
Jackie Shelford, Shelter, Mark Stevens,
and Tim Walker.

Contents

The Authors

Graham Roberts is a postgraduate researching for a D Phil at Sussex University. His special interest is the Soviet Union. A late entrant to full-time further education, he worked for one year in a bank and seven years later as a librarian, studying three years part-time and at the Open University. He graduated from Kingston Polytechnic in 1986 with an honours degree in History and Politics and obtained an MA in History at Sussex in 1987.

Andrew Moore graduated from Lancaster University in 1974 with an honours degree in Economics and Financial Control. He joined the staff of a major clearing bank, working in provincial and city branches as well as its head office. A writer with an international audience, he now writes on a variety of subjects ranging from personal finance to the arts. He has regular columns in six countries and is currently writing a book on the Fabergé family.

Theoretically it is possible to write a cheque on anything.

Foreword

GRAHAM ROBERTS AND ANDREW MOORE have, between them, filled an important gap in the relatively new, but rapidly expanding, market for guides to personal finances.

This book is well thought out and on each test of such books it fits the bill. It is *needed* because there is no equivalent, for while NUS publishes a detailed annual guide for student advisers, the NUS *Welfare Manual*, there is no guide for the layperson. *The Student Money Guide* is readable and comprehensible, and it is accurate – in stark contrast to many of the guides to students published in magazines every autumn.

The Student Money Guide has an additional, and commendable, quality. It is dynamic, approaching rules and regulations from the point of view of the student and the parent, rather than expecting the reader to relate obscure regulations to their own situation.

For this reason the book fulfils another function. It is possible to understand *how* students live, their problems and how they can overcome them. People talk about students as if they were an isolated group when, in fact, the recent changes in social security and housing policy, not to mention the poll tax, all have profound effects on students.

For all this, the Government's plans to introduce 'top-up' loans and end student entitlement to social security benefit from 1990 seem all the more remarkable. Ministers and many of the loans 'experts' who queue up outside the television studios to give their considered opinions about student financial support would do well to read this book.

Sarah Adams,
Vice-President of the National Union of Students

CHAPTER 1

Introduction

*'Education is a sieve as well
as a ladder.'*

Sid Chaplin

OVER THE last five years, we have been writing on the subject of student finance and there is no doubt that over this period, it has become increasingly more difficult for those at university, college or polytechnic to make their financial resources stretch to meet all the needs of student life. This book will not resolve the situation, but it will help prevent any financial disasters.

Consideration of the financial aspects when planning to start a course of further education should start well before the beginning of term. At the forefront of most parents' minds is the grant situation. The most frequently encountered question, not unreasonably, is, 'How much am I expected to contribute?' As many aspects of the grant system as is practical are dealt with, but not every situation can be examined. Eligibility for a grant is covered and the book outlines the procedure for applying for a grant. Although the regulations regarding grants are complex and not all of the 1989–90 allowances are available at the time of going to press, guidance is given as to how to calculate roughly the level of maintenance grant the authorities will pay and the sum parents will be expected to pay.

Student finance is not just about giving advice to those who actually undertake a course of further education. While it is generally appreciated that students can suffer financial difficulties, it is easy to forget that parents may be hardpressed to find the money to pay towards their offsprings' living expenses. Most parents enjoy a regular income but in situations where the parental contribution is a high proportion (not to mention total) part of a student's resources during the academic year, the parental dues at the beginning of each term are high. The book discusses the various sources of finance for parents who find themselves in the position of having to make large irregular payments out of a regular income. This is a situation which the means-test of the parents' income completely overlooks.

Another important issue is the subject of student loans. Prior to the publication of the White Paper, *Top-Up Loans for Students*, there was great speculation in the press as to what the Government proposed. Ever since its publication a controversy has raged as to whether or not the proposals are workable. As one economic commentator remarked, the 'publication is more green that white, since it leaves so many options open and so many issues of implementation unresolved' (**Lloyds Bank Economic Bulletin**). To quote some of the headlines:

*NUS sets up 'hotline' on student loan fears . . . Student loans 'trap poor' . . . Baker seeks new bank for student loans . . . Banks angered by pressure to fund £400 student loans . . . Americans to step in over student loans . . . Tory MPs unhappy at student loans plan . . . Clash as 20,000 protest over student loan plan . . . Bankers grapple with student loans . . . Universities 'should run loan scheme' . . . Vice Chancellors reject proposals for student loans . . . Banks poised to support loan scheme for students (**Financial Times**, 28 December 1988). Banks still cool on student loans (**Guardian**, 28 December 1988) Student loans 'to cost more than savings' . . . Why the Government is wrong on student loans: it would be cheaper to give the money away . . . Big banks dismiss student loan plan . . . Baker moves to break bank stalemate . . . Student loan plan in trouble.*

Although we cannot speculate as to what is going to happen, the book outlines the Government proposals and the main concerns. The only thing that can be said with certainty is that the whole saga will be an ideal research project for some future historian.

The most usual form of financial disagreement between parents and their offspring is caused by a lack of communication. Both students and their parents should discuss frankly what the financial implications are before a course of further education is started. The earlier this is done the better. Parents should state what they are prepared to contribute and when. Students should give thought as to how much is ideally required for living expenses, remembering that the ideal and reality do not always coincide. However, parents and students who work together as a team and who recognise that there are problems on both sides, are far more likely to survive in harmony over a three-year period than those who completely ignore the difficulties faced by the other party.

Although the cost of living in particular circumstances cannot be included, guidance is given as to how to obtain the likely costs. While some of the advice is mainly applicable to students who live away from home, most aspects are equally as important to those who reside with their parents. For example, over-enthusiasm for buying books should be resisted. The book lists issued before or at the start of term are generally long. However, they are recommended reading lists, not lists of compulsory buys. At the end of term, when funds may be low, there is nothing worse than looking at un-opened books on a shelf. General advice on possible economies is given, insuring personal effects, part-time jobs, the student tax position; the book warns against being pressurised into taking out whole-life insurance policies which most students cannot afford, or indeed require. Much of the advice passed on has been gleaned from students nationwide. It is therefore practical as opposed to theoretical.

By far the largest section in the book is devoted to

banking. The book shows how to choose a bank, open an account, and how to operate it to the best advantage. Aspects such as what to do if a cheque book, cheque card, cash card or credit card goes missing are covered. In the event of a grant cheque being late, the text outlines the procedure to follow.

Borrowing money is also dealt with. The cheapest sources of funds are outlined and advice is given on how to impress a bank manager when asking to borrow money. There is also a gentle reminder that money lent has to be repaid and that credit cards can damage wealth!

The mysteries of the workings of banks are also revealed and tips are given regarding general financial security – and the possible consequences if simple rules are not observed.

Undoubtedly one of the keys to students' finances running smoothly is planning. Budgeting can take many forms. It does not matter which approach is adopted, as long as some form of financial planning is undertaken. Budgeting itself does not create money, but it at least indicates what can and what cannot be done. Once a budget has been formulated it must be monitored and action taken when danger signs are spotted. Finally, although it is hoped that none of our readers will find themselves in the position, guidance is given as to the courses of action to take if finances do collapse into a hopeless mess.

A course of further education is not just about obtaining an academic qualification, but it is also a study of life. For many students it will be their first taste of independence away from home. A whole new social and academic world will open. The object of this book is to give those embarking upon university, college or polytechnic courses practical financial advice. If financial problems can be avoided there is every likelihood that the course will be far more enjoyable. To quote Peter Ustinov: *'British education is probably the best in the world, if you can survive it.'*

CHAPTER 2

Student Loans

'Inflation is one form of taxation that can be imposed without legislation'

Milton Friedman

IN 1987 the Government published its response to the House of Commons' Education, Science and Arts Committee, Session 1986–87 on Student Awards. It is interesting to note the following extract.

> As a result of the welcome increase in student numbers the pressures on the funds available for student support have been growing for many years: it is now doubtful whether the present arrangements can provide a fully satisfactory long-term system of support for students' maintenance without a larger call on public funds than it is reasonable to expect the taxpayer to meet. The problem was anticipated by Lord Robbins in his discussion of loans in 1963: 'At a time when many parents are only just beginning to acquire the habit of contemplating higher education for such of their children, especially girls, as are capable of benefiting by it, we think it probable that [loans] would have undesirable disincentive effects. But if, as time goes on, the habit is more firmly established, the arguments of justice in distribution and of the advantage of increasing individual responsibility may come to weigh more heavily and lead to some experiment in this direction ...'

On 9 November 1988, the Government introduced its

proposals concerning the future arrangements for student support. The White Paper is entitled *Top-up Loans for Students.*

The Government's proposals

Objectives

The White Paper sets out the main purposes of the scheme, which are:

- to share the cost of students' maintenance more equitably between students, parents and the taxpayer;
- to increase the resources available to students;
- to reduce the contribution to students' maintenance which is expected from parents;
- to reduce direct public expenditure on grants;
- to reduce students dependency by removing them from the Social Security benefits system;
- to increase economic awareness and self-reliance among students.

Summary of the proposals

In brief, the Government's proposals as published in the White Paper involve:

- from the academic year 1990–91, a loan facility, at nil real interest, of up to £460 according to place of residence during term for each *full* academic year, with a loan of up to £340 in the student's financial year;
- the grant and parental contribution to be frozen from 1990–91;
- the loan portion of the student maintenance grant to be increased each year until it is equal to the value of the grant and parental contribution taken together;
- repayment of the loan will be deferred when a graduate's income is low;
- from 1990–91 full-time students will no longer be eligible for income support, unemployment benefit, or housing benefits;

- disabled students, students who are single parents, and partners of students will remain eligible for benefits, and support for students' dependents will also continue;
- the Government will establish three 'access' or charitable funds to provide discretionary support in individual cases of financial need for students losing their entitlement to benefits:
  - (i) for students within the scope of the new loans regime
  - (ii) for postgraduates
  - (iii) for students in further education.

The Government subsequently announced that the parental contribution scale will be re-indexed annually. The basis for the change will not be the retail prices index since incomes have recently tended to rise more rapidly. It also announced that there would be a final increase in grants for the academic year 1990–91.

What the proposals mean

Loans will be available to all full-time students up to the age of 50. Students will still be entitled to the portion of the grant available within the system. The actual amount which can be borrowed will depend upon the place of residence.

TABLE 1
THE INITIAL PROPOSED LOAN SCHEME

	Full year	**Final year**
Hall or lodgings	*Maximum loan (£)*	*Maximum loan (£)*
London	*460*	*340*
Elsewhere	*420*	*310*
Parental home any location	*330*	*240*

From 1990–91 the Government will freeze grants and index-link the parental contribution scales. Parental contributions will not be abolished. The amounts to be borrowed are, of course, maximum amounts and parents may contribute more to their offsprings' living costs, thus requiring their sons and daughters to borrow less. The loan scheme will not eliminate students dependence on banks for their short-term borrowing needs.

We are grateful to the National Union of Students (NUS) for permission to reproduce material from its Parents' Pack, *Grants Not Loans*, published towards the end of 1988, which outlines the NUS's views as to the effect of the proposed scheme.

Repayments

The outstanding debt acquired by students will be adjusted in line with inflation; as inflation rises, so does the amount to be paid back. Liability to repay will begin nine months after a student has completed his or her course.

The White Paper presents a series of options for repayment regimes:

- *a repayment period over a fixed number of years (say, ten) with the amount paid by each individual per month varying depending on how much they have borrowed; or*
- *a variable repayment period with fixed annual instalments. This would mean those with small loans would complete their payments quickly, while those with a greater debts would take longer to pay it off; or*
- *the repayment period could be determined by the size of the debt; or*
- *the level of instalments could be varied depending on the income of the graduate.*

The White Paper states that no payments would be required below a certain income. This would not diminish the debt, which would continue to grow as interest was added.

Access funds

As well as establishing the loans system, the Government intends to set up three Access or 'Charity' funds. These funds will have £5 millions each and are intended to provide help to those most in need within the loans system, to further education students and for post-graduates. The college will be required to submit bids for their allocation of funds. To quote from the White Paper.

The Government hopes that the institutions will themselves work out imaginative arrangements for enhancing the value and scope of the funds, for example by linking payments to sponsorship, helping students to find paid employment or making some payments on a repayable basis, as well as making grants.

Will students be better off with loans?

Under the present grants system, students have four main sources of income:

- *the grant from their Local Education Authority (LEA);*
- *the contribution to the grant from their parents;*
- *Housing benefit from the local council to help pay the rent; and*
- *Income support from the Department of Social Security (DSS) over the summer holidays for students who cannot find jobs.*

Under the proposed system the total amount a student receives in the form of a grant will be frozen and parental contribution will be index-linked. Students will be able to obtain a loan, but the Government will take away the main welfare benefits (housing benefit and income support) from all full-time students except single parents and disabled students. This means that during the academic year (the three terms plus the two short vacations) many students will have less income after housing costs than is the case at present.

The academic year
In the academic year 1986–87 the average student rent was £21 a week outside London. Students paying such a rent would have about £4.50 a week more income under the loans proposals.

However, rents in many areas are much higher. In the South East rents are around £30 per week, sometimes higher. Such students will be over £4.50 a week worse off, a loss of over £172 over the academic year.

However, by 1990 rents will have continued their upward trends. Rents all over the country will be higher, so virtually all students will lose out.

In London, where the average rent was £35 in 1986–87, but rents are often as high as £50 a week students will lose out more heavily.

The long vacation
During the summer, students who cannot find jobs and who are available for work, can claim income support from the DSS. This is worth £27.40 a week for a single student aged under 25 and £34.90 for those aged over 25.

Students who receive income support also receive housing benefit which covers all the rent. Many students have to pay rent over the summer to secure accommodation for the next academic year. This is because landlords will only let accommodation on a 52-week basis.

Under the proposed system, the only resources provided for students is a loan of £110 (or £120 in London) for the summer vacation. This is not even enough to pay for the lowest rents.

While it is true that many students find work over the summer, many cannot find work, especially if they are living in areas of high unemployment. Very few students find work for the whole period of the vacation. Other students undertake voluntary work over the summer vacation – sometimes as part of college-run schemes. Even these students will not receive any support from the Government.

It is clear that the Government intends all students to

return to their parental home for the summer vacation, and expects their parents to support them for this period.

How the proposals affect parents

It is claimed that the proposals in the White Paper will substantially ease the burden on parents. A closer look at the scheme reveals that quite the opposite will occur.

NUS is aware of the concern expressed by many parents that the loans will be compulsory. This is not in fact the case and consequently some parents may feel a moral pressure to pay over and above their expected contribution so that their children can avoid falling into debt.

Surveys of students income and expenditure show that while many parents do not or cannot afford to pay their full contribution, a substantial proportion pay significantly more than is required. This is clearly a recognition of the shortfall in students' resources.

The figure produced by NUS clearly demonstrates that these proposals, far from meeting that shortfall in resources, will actually exacerbate it in many cases. With no system of welfare benefits available to students, many will be forced to turn to their parents as the only remaining source of support.

The withdrawal of benefit entitlement over the summer months is particularly disturbing. It will be almost impossible to retain rented accommodation during this period. It is clear that the loans scheme has been devised with the expectation that all students can and do return to their parental home to be supported over the summer months.

In the experience of NUS this is simply not the case. It is important that students do have minimal resources available to them during this time because many families cannot support them.

The White Paper claims that the scheme proposed will 'increase the economic awareness of students, and their self-reliance'. In fact the White Paper takes as its starting point the assumption that students are dependant on their parents and can rely on them for assistance when they are in financial difficulty. These proposals will not provide relief for parents but will instead foster and entrench the relationship of financial dependancy of students on their parents.

The NUS will issue revised editions of its *Parents Pack, Grants Not Loans* if the proposals change.

Events since the publication of the proposals

The White Paper has not exactly been warmly welcomed. Indeed, it appears to have few supporters outside the Department of Education and Science and HM Treasury. When Kenneth Baker, Education Secretary, made his statement to the House of Commons on 9 November 1989, he said: 'In the Government's view, the top-up loan scheme is best administered by the financial institutions. I am now embarking on discussions with them.'

Here are a selection of press reports from our cuttings file. They adequately reflect developments.

Banks attack Government over student loan plans

Bankers gave a hostile reception yesterday to the Government's plans to introduce student loans, which they will have the task of administering. Several banks said they were reluctant to support the scheme as outlined in a White Paper on Wednesday.

The Committee of London and Scottish Bankers, the clearing banks' trade association, said: 'You could say that the banks are not exactly jumping up and down with delight at this.'

One clearing bank official went so far as to say: 'There is no interest in this for the banks. We think it is unworkable', adding that the banks' co-operation seemed to have been taken for granted ...

Bankers are also opposed to the manner in which the scheme will be run. The Government will make the loans and pay the banks to administer them, possibly on the basis of competitive tendering ...

Bankers were also worried about who would have responsibility for chasing up student loan defaulters.

The banks, rather than the Government, would be blamed for any failings in the scheme ...

The student loan market is a particularly sensitive one for the banks because it represents the source of future business ...

Bankers are unlikely to press their objections to the point where they scupper the scheme.

Financial Times, *11 November 1988*

NUS sets up 'hotline' on student loan fears

The NUS is setting up a 'hotline' today to deal with enquiries from students and parents who are worried about government proposals to introduce a system of student loans.

A spokesman said the union had received a flood of telephone calls since the proposal for loans to top-up the student grant was unveiled in a White Paper last Wednesday ...

A union spokesman said yesterday, 'Many of the calls received have only been for clarification of what is being proposed. But a high level of concern has been raised about the effects on parental contributions and the loss of entitlement to welfare benefits.

The Times, *14 November 1988*

Baker seeks new bank for student loans

- *Ministers are considering a tie-up with Girobank or an overseas lender to implement their student loan proposals.*
- *The big High Street banks are reluctant to respond to the scheme announced last week by Mr Kenneth Baker ...*
- *If all else fails, the Department of Education and Science may have to resort to the Treasury for help.*

The Times, *18 November 1988*

Banks angered by pressure to fund £400 student loans

The four main clearing banks last night brushed

aside ministerial suggestions of a tie-up with Giro-bank or an overseas lender to implement a student loans package.

Privately, senior figures in the banks were highly critical of what was seen as a crude attempt to persuade them to drop their opposition to the scheme ...

The Times, *19 November 1988*

Tory MPs unhappy at student loans plan

Clear warnings of Conservative backbench disquiet against government proposals to introduce student loans emerged last night with a strong attack on the plan by Mr Robert Rhodes James, MP for Cambridge.

Another Tory MP, Mr Robert McCrinde (Ongar), supported the scheme unveiled by Mr Baker, Education Secretary, earlier this month – but doubted that it would 'get off the ground' ...

Daily Telegraph, *24 November 1988*

Clash as 20,000 protest over loans scheme

Mounted police wielding batons yesterday dispersed a student demonstration after thousands of protestors broke away from a march, brought London to a standstill for hours and confronted police as they tried to reach parliament ...

The Times, *25 November 1988*

Vice chancellors reject proposals for student loans

Britain's university vice chancellors yesterday rejected the Government's proposals for a system of top-up loans and decided instead to try to devise a better scheme themselves.

They are also likely to consider a proposal from Professor John Ashworth, vice chancellor of Salford University, that the universities should seek to administer the loan scheme in place of the banks and building societies that the Government envisages as administrators ...

Financial Times, *10 December 1988*

Banks poised to support loan scheme for students

Britain's high street banks appear ready to drop their opposition to the student loan scheme planned by the Government, and may set up an organisation run jointly by the financial institutions to administer the loans ...

Financial Times, 28 December 1988

Banks still cool on student loans

Education ministers are working on an alternative to the scheme for student loans in the face of continued resistance to the plan by banks and financial institutions.

Banking sources yesterday insisted, in the face of newspaper reports to the contrary, that they still had reservations about the proposal under which financial institutions would administer repayments of top-up loans given to every undergraduate by the Treasury.

Guardian, 29 December 1988

Student loans 'to cost more than savings'

Annual costs of administering the Government's proposed student loan package will outstrip the total long-term savings projected for the scheme, according to a report commissioned by the Higher Education Minister, Mr Robert Jackson.

The claim casts doubt over the viability of existing proposals at a time when the High Street banks are undecided on whether to back the project.

The author of the paper said yesterday it would be cheaper to give students the money as grants.

Dr Nicholas Barr of the London School of Economics argues in his paper **Student Loans: The Next Steps** *that, within five years, estimated administration costs of recouping loans would amount to £100 per student per annum, totalling £50 million for those students currently in higher education.*

However, this figure would be boosted each year as new generations of graduates come into the system and, *Dr Barr says, 'the costs could easily reach £250 million . . .'*

Dr Barr, a lecturer in economics, was asked to write the paper after two meetings with Mr Jackson in which he argued that loans should be repaid through National Insurance Contributions.

This would make administration easier, keeping costs to around £10 million a year, and reduce the scope for default.

The Government last year rejected this approach because it wanted loans administered by private banking institutions.

Sunday Telegraph, *1 January 1988*

Baker moves to break bank stalemate

A move aimed at persuading one of the high street banks or another financial institution to steal a march on its rivals and support the Government's top-up student loan scheme is being planned by Mr Kenneth Baker.

After months of fruitless negotiations with a group representing the clearing banks and building societies, the Secretary of State for Education and Science has decided to break the deadlock by talking directly to possible partners.

The Times, *27 January 1989*

Student loan plans 'should be scrapped'

The Government should scrap its proposals for student loans and instead introduce a system of giving parents tax relief on loans to cover student mainte-nance according to Mr Christopher Johnson, chief economic adviser to Lloyds Bank.

Mr Johnson is highly critical of the proposals for subsidised commercial loans.

Mr Johnson's paper reflects the irritation felt by the high street banks at the Department of Education and

Science's failure to consult them fully before its scheme was published.

Financial Times, *6 February 1989*

The eventual scheme

It is unlikely that the Government anticipated so much opposition to its proposals for its student loan scheme. What will transpire, if indeed anything, is completely unknown at the time of writing. Developments will be reported in the press and NUS will issue information regarding the effects of any changes to the proposals.

Inflation is one form of taxation that can be imposed without legislation.

CHAPTER 3

Grants

*'If you think education is
expensive, try ignorance.'*

Derek Bok

THE STATUTORY INSTRUMENT detailing the complexities
of the student grant system is published each
summer. The Education (Mandatory Awards) Regulations 1988 comprised of 33 pages and was available from
HMSO at £4.50. The Regulations are written in a legal
language and make difficult reading.

This chapter briefly outlines the grant system. As
with all guides, it is not possible to cover every situation.
However, by working through this chapter it will be
possible to ascertain if an individual student is eligible
for a grant and, if so, roughly how much is likely to be
received. Also dealt with is the emotive issue of the
parental contribution.

Before proceeding further, the definition of words
frequently used, should be explained. The Regulations
have awards in their title, yet everyone refers to grants.
Whilst the two words are used interchangeably, the
Regulations distinguish between the two:

- an award comprises two elements;
    - (i) the tuition fees paid direct to the educational
      establishment;
    - (ii) a maintenance payment to the student for accom-
      modation, food, books, etc;
- a grant is the maintenance payment in (ii) above.

The title of the Regulations stipulates mandatory
awards. There are two types of award:

- *mandatory* – Local Education Authorities (LEAS) are obliged to make such awards to students who:
  (i) undertake 'designated' courses;
  (ii) are personally eligible for the award.

Designated courses and eligibility are dealt with below.

- *discretionary* – students who do not undertake designated courses, or who undertake such a course but are not eligible for a mandatory award, *may* qualify for a discretionary grant. Details are given on page 26.

Mandatory awards

Designated courses
In almost all cases, designated courses are full-time or sandwich courses, although certain part-time initial teacher training courses are designated for grant purposes. Designated courses are mainly those leading to:

- first degree provided by a UK university, the Cranfield Institute, or under the aegis of the Council for National Academic Awards. (*Note:* First degree courses provided jointly by an establishment in the UK and an overseas establishment are designated.);
- diploma of higher education;
- higher national diploma (HND).

together with the following:

- courses of initial teacher training, part-time day courses of teacher training which are designated by the Secretary of State (including the Postgraduate Certificate of Education);
- courses provided by a university leading to a certificate, diploma or other academic qualification comparable to a first degree, provided that the course is of at least three years' duration;
- other qualifications which are specifically designated as being comparable to a first degree course. Qualifications in this category are listed in *Designated courses* obtainable from LEAS or direct from the

Department of Education and Science, Room 8/1, Elizabeth House, York Road, London SE1 7PH.

Personal eligibility

The fact that an individual has been accepted for a designated course does not necessarily mean that a mandatory award will be forthcoming. In addition, the student must be personally eligible. Although the final decision regarding eligibility rests with LEAs, the following is a guide for individual qualification:

Residency

To satisfy the following residency requirements in order to qualify for a mandatory award applicants must:

(a) have been ordinarily resident in the British islands (ie the UK, Channel Islands or the Isle of Man) for three years prior to 1 September, 1 January or 1 April whichever is closest to the start of the course, according to whether it begins in the autumn or summer term; and

(b) the purpose of residence during *any* of that three year period must not have been wholly or mainly to receive full-time education.

However, there are exceptions to the three year rule:

(i) Students who are or were not ordinarily resident in the UK only because they, or their spouse or parents are or were temporarily employed outside the British Isles.
The Department of Education and Science's (DES) Publications Dispatch Centre – see *Addresses of Useful Contacts* on page 165 – publishes a supplementary fact sheet about awards for UK citizens working overseas. Each LEA determines what is 'temporary employment overseas'. Those students still abroad can contact the LEA in the area where they were ordinarily resident in the UK.

(ii) Students from other member states of the European Community who can establish 'migrant worker' status, or whose parents are migrant workers.

(iii) UK-recognised refugees or asylees, their spouses or children.

Previous courses

The candidate must not have attended a course of advanced further education for more than two years (this does *not* include A-levels or their equivalent).

Abandoned courses are disregarded, provided attendance was for no more than one term and seven weeks of the second term.

The rule regarding previous courses in excess of two years is very strict. There is no time limit as to when the course was undertaken. Additionally, even courses for which no award was previously made are not disregarded. Indeed, even further education studies undertaken abroad count as a 'previous course'. There are only two exceptions:

- students who successfully apply for a Postgraduate Certificate of education course who have a first degree;
- students who have previously received bursaries for courses at long-term residential colleges (eg Ruskin College).

If a further education course of up to two years has previously been undertaken, the amount of the mandatory award may be reduced, unless the subsequent course is a BEd in a 'shortage subject', ie chemistry, maths (or a combination of the two subjects), craft, design and technology; business studies or a course which the area LEA considers has scope for the applicant to teach one of these subjects.

With the exception of the BEds previously outlined, the award will be reduced if the previous course was:

- a designated course of up to two years; or
- a non-designated course of exactly two years.

The amount of the award is reduced by restricting the years in which it will be forthcoming for the new course:

- where its normal duration is two years or less, in respect of the final year only;
- where its normal duration is more than two years, to the final year or years after deducting two years from its normal duration.

For example, this means that a student who has completed a two-year HND course and then wishes to proceed to a three-year degree course, will only gain a mandatory award in the final year of the new course. Similarly, if the same student wishes to proceed to a four-year degree, the award would only be given for the *final* two years of the degree course. A discretionary award could be paid during those years when a mandatory award is not given.

Application must be made on time

Applications must be made by the end of the first term to the LEA in whose area the student was ordinarily resident on the last day of June, February or October, according to whether the academic year of the course commenced in the autumn, spring or summer respectively. In other words, for a course beginning in September/October, the applicable date where the applicant was ordinarily resident would be 30 June. Although the application need not be made until the end of the first term (ie December), applications should be forwarded sooner rather than later. Most LEAs will begin to accept applications from the end of January for a course starting in the autumn. Students should not wait until examination results are available, but apply as soon as possible after a provisional place has been secured on the chosen course.

Important points to note:

- failure to apply on time will result in no mandatory award for the whole course;
- the later you apply, the greater the risk of the first grant cheque being late;
- if there is any doubt as to which is your local LEA (eg

an impending family move), send a photocopy of the main application to other possible LEAs together with a covering letter, asking what area each covers;
- if the application deadline is missed, the university or college can always be asked to hold the place over for a year. Although 12 months will have been lost, the award will not have been lost.

Applications are dealt with in depth on pages 43-45.

Student conduct

It is rare for an award to be declined due to conduct but it is always a possibility. If an applicant is, in the opinion of the LEA processing the application, 'unfitting to hold an award', the LEA is not obliged to grant one. The phrase is not defined in the Regulations.

Assisted students

The applicant must not be an 'assisted student', in other words an individual who has been given paid leave from employment to attend the course. Typical examples are armed forces cadets. Students in receipt of a scholarship or who receive payments from a sponsoring employer are not 'assisted students', providing the sum paid does not exceed (1989-90) £2750.

Discretionary awards

All may not be lost if you do not qualify for a mandatory award as LEAs have the power to make awards at their discretion.

It must be stated at the outset that each LEA has its own policy regarding discretionary awards. It is therefore essential not to be over-optimistic regarding individual circumstances. Although general guidelines cannot be given, it is a recognised fact that discretionary awards are sometimes competitive. In other words, examination results are taken into consideration. This is not the case where mandatory awards are concerned. There is also a further difference. The place of study is not a factor which is taken into consideration where mandatory awards are concerned but this is not necessarily so with discretionary awards. An LEA may adopt the policy that it will only assist if a course is local.

The amount of a discretionary award for a designated course will be calculated according to the Regulations for a mandatory award. However, if a discretionary award is made for a non-designated course, the value of the award is entirely discretionary.

As the sum each LEA sets aside for discretionary awards may be small, it is strongly advised to apply as early as possible. Write to your LEA giving full details. A *curriculum vitae* should be attached so that your academic achievements can be seen 'at a glance'. Include your grades for all examination passes.

Calculating the amount of a mandatory award

Those who qualify for a mandatory award will always have their tuition fees paid direct by their LEA to the educational establishment at which they are to study. Students who are classed as being independent of their parents will receive a maintenance grant, the exact amount payable being determined by a means test of the student's and his/her spouse's income. As will be outlined later, 'independent student' is clearly defined in the Regulations. No student can declare himself or herself independent of their parents. Students deemed dependent of their parents will receive a maintenance grant, the exact amount payable being determined by a means-test on both the student's and parents' income.

Basic grants

The main rates of undergraduate grants in the UK for the 1989 academic year were announced on 16 December 1988. For the first time ever, the grant for London increased proportionately more than the other rates, thus indicating that the financial plight of those studying in London is being recognised by those at the Department of Education and Science. Grants in general increased by an average of 5 per cent whilst the London rate increased by 9.3 per cent.

TABLE 2
BASIC GRANTS

Accommodation	England, Wales & Northern Ireland	Scotland
	Maximum (£)	*Maximum (£)*
Hall or lodgings		
London	*2650*	*2585*
Elsewhere	*2155*	*2090*
Parental home		
Any location	*1710*	*1575*

Note: *Scotland's basic grant is lower as travel costs above the first £55 are reclaimable, whereas elsewhere, students receive a fixed amount as part of their maintenance grant irrespective of their travel costs.*

Students cannot opt to live away from the parental home and claim the larger hall or lodgings grant if there is no reason why they should not lodge with their parents during the course. Generally, any maintenance grant will be based on the *parental home grant* of £1710 (or £1575 in Scotland) unless:

- the student lives in college accommodation;
- it is the LEA's view that the student cannot 'conveniently attend' the course whilst based at the parental home;
- the student already lives away from home and has independent status or is married.

Students who attend a course of further education in the UK and who are required to study overseas for at least one term, will receive a grant based on the 'overseas' scale. The amount of the maximum grant depends on the country being visited and is subject to means-testing. The figures quoted in table 3 are for the standard academic year. Payments for portions of an academic year will be on a pro-rata basis. At the time of writing the 1989-90 figures for Scotland are not available.

TABLE 3
OVERSEAS STUDY GRANTS

Country	England, Wales & Northern Ireland (£)	Scotland (£)
Highest cost countries *Finland, Japan, Norway and* USA	3330*	3110
Higher cost countries *Australia, Canada, Denmark, Eire, France, West Germany, Netherlands, Sweden and Switzerland*	2935*	2735
High cost countries *Belgium, Hong Kong, Indonesia, Italy, Luxembourg and* USSR	2545*	2365
All other countries	2155*	1990

* 1989-90 rates are shown by use of asterisks.

Further information regarding overseas study is available from LEAS. Also see travelling expenses on page 34.

Additional allowances
The Regulations also make provision for 'supplementary maintenance requirements'. These extra allowances are for additional course attendance, travelling expenses, mature and disabled students. At the time of writing not all of the 1989-90 allowances are available.

Extra weeks attendance
The basic grant covers a standard academic year of 30 weeks and 3 days or in the case of Cambridge and Oxford universities 25 weeks and 3 days. An additional payment is made for each week's required attendance above the standard periods given above.

TABLE 4
PAYMENTS FOR REQUIRED EXTRA ATTENDANCE

Place of Residence	England, Wales & Northern Ireland	Scotland
	£ per week	£ per week
London—excluding parental home	60.15*	51.30
Elsewhere—excluding parental home	45.05*	39.10
Parental Home	31.55*	23.95
Highest cost countries	83.35*	75.40
Higher cost countries	70.60*	63.50
High cost countries	57.80*	51.30
All other countries	45.05*	39.10

* 1989-90 rates.

Students required to attend their course for 45 weeks or more in any 12-month period will receive a grant for all

52 weeks of the year. All payments for extra weeks are means-tested.

Travelling expenses

The major difference between the grant system in Scotland and elsewhere in the UK is the method of making provision for travelling expenses.

Travelling expenses: England, Wales and Northern Ireland

New arrangements were introduced for the academic year commencing in September 1984. Since that date all new students generally receive no help with travel costs beyond the fixed element included in the basic grant. The 1989-90 figure is £190 for students residing at their parental home and £120 for those living elsewhere. There are only three exceptions to this rule. Students receive full reimbursement for travel expenditure over the fixed element included in the basic grant only in the following situations:

- disabled students provided the additional costs are incurred as a result of their disability;
- students who attend, as a necessary part of their UK course, an institution overseas;
- students who attend, as a necessary part of their medical, dentistry or nursing course, a place in the UK away from their main educational establishment, eg a hospital for clinical training.

Payments will be within limits which LEAs consider to be 'reasonable' payments. In other words, students will be expected to take advantage of any concessionary fares available.

Travelling expenses: Scotland

Scottish maintenance grants include an allowance for travel costs of £55. Students can, within limits, claim travel expenses in excess of this sum from the Scottish Education Department. Eligible travel includes return journeys from parental homes to the term-time address by the most economic fare (where this is through the

Railcard the cost of the card can also be claimed), plus daily travel to college, limited to a maximum of £2.40 a day. A maximum level of claim is set which is equal to the difference between the 'parental home' and 'hall or lodgings' elsewhere rates. The maximum additional travel reimbursement for 1989-90 is £515.

Disabled students

The 1989-90 Regulations will allow disabled students to claim an additional allowance of £765 if, by reason of their disability, they were obliged to incur additional expenditure as a result of attendance on the course. The rule relates to students in all parts of Britain.

It is important to note that the allowance is a maximum amount and not a sum that a LEA will pay in every case. It is interesting to note the NUS's *Welfare Manual 1988/9* regarding the disabled student allowance:

> *The positive aspect is that it does not prescribe a list of situations under which the allowance is claimable, and therefore means that each case can be looked at on its merits. The negative side is that some LEAs take a very narrow view as to whether the particular additional expenditure is incurred as a result of the student's disability and their attendance on the course. The DES in their notes for guidance state that: 'Claims up to the maximum entitlement on items and expenses such as tape recorders for the blind; special equipment for the handicapped; the use of readers and amanuenses where necessary and other extra aids might be met as part of the allowances. Handicapped students may also have other expenses over and above those incurred by others; it would not be unreasonable for example to expect a visually handicapped student to make more use of the telephone. In some cases students may also face, as a result of a disability, higher heating or dietary expenses than if they were not on the course (for instance where these were paid for in the normal place of residence before the course began).*

Justified and quantified claims in respect of such additional sums may also be met from the allowance up to the maximum amount prescribed, provided they are related both to disability and to attendance on the course.'

Mature students

It is not only old age pensioners who receive an age allowance. However, a student does not have to be a senior citizen in order to qualify. An additional payment – up to £840 for 1989-90 – is payable to students aged 26 or more. However, there is a proviso. In order to qualify for the allowance, students must have earned, or received in taxable unemployment or income support, at least £12000 during the three years prior to the commencement of the course.

The allowance covers 52 weeks of the year. The amount actually received is dependent on the student's age. The 1989-90 allowances are:

TABLE 5
MATURE STUDENTS' ADDITIONAL GRANT

Age	£
26	240
27	435
28	645
29+	840

The parental contribution

The Government's White Paper *Top-Up Loans for Students* was published in November 1988. It neatly summarises an aspect of the current grant system that parents generally dread:

The parental contribution is based upon the parents' residual income; the income of both parents is taken into account in its calculation. Residual income is defined as the parents' gross income in the preceding financial year less certain deductions, chiefly for other adult dependents, interest payments (including mortgage interest), superannuation, life insurance and pension scheme contributions. After residual income has been calculated, and the parental contribution assessed, further deductions are made in respect of any other dependent children of the family.

About 12 per cent of mandatory award holders are independent of their parents (see below). Government research has revealed that about 30 per cent of dependent students receive the maintenance grant in full. The others have their grant abated for a parental contribution, with the result that nearly 25 per cent receive no maintenance grant at all. The White Paper states, 'the parental contribution begins to bear on families where incomes are a little more than the national average.' It illustrates the point with the following chart.

CHART 1
PARENTAL CONTRIBUTION COMPARED TO GROSS INCOME

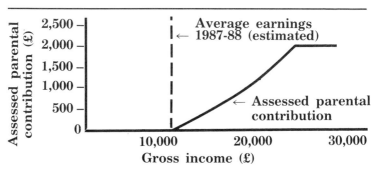

1 Chart based on the new contribution scale for 1988-89 for parents without covenants, and on the hypothesis of one child in the family.
2 Residual income is taken to equal approximately 90 per cent of gross income.

Source: Top-Up Loans for Students, November 1980, HMSO.

Independent students

Only students who are classed as independent will not have their award means-tested with regard to their parents' income. An independent student is a person who:

- has reached the age of 25 years before the start of the academic year for which the grant is being assessed;
- is an orphan;
- has been married for at least two years prior to the commencement of the academic year;
- has been self-supporting for *any* three years prior to the course. 'Self-support' can include:
  (i) any period of unemployment,
  (ii) any period for which the student was in receipt of sickness benefit, invalidity pension, severe disablement or maternity allowance,
  (iii) any period of TOPS, YOPS, or YTS training.

A parental contribution will also not be assessed in the following situations if the students' parents:

- cannot be found;
- it is not practicable to get in touch with them;
- reside overseas and the assessment of a contribution would place them in jeopardy (eg the student is a refugee);
- the student has been in the care of a local authority or voluntary organisation;
- the student has been subject to a custodianship order for the three years immediately preceding his or her 18th birthday, or immediately preceding the course if he or she is not 18 years old when it commenced.

Note: A student who has not been married for two years or 'self-supporting' for three years and who is not yet 25 years old and does not meet any other criteria to satisfy independent student status, will have the award assessed on his or her parents' income. This subject is covered in a later section in this chapter on page 42.

The parental residual income

In the above section it was stated that residual income is defined as the parents' gross income in the preceding financial year less certain deductions. This means that the income when calculating residual income for a course starting in the autumn of 1989 is earnings, commission, bonuses, profits, rents, dividends, interest received – ie total taxable income – in the 1988-89 tax year. The authorities realise that it is not always fair to expect parents to pay their contribution on an assessment of last year's revenue out of current net income. Consequently, there are exceptions to the general rule. For example:

1 *Income from business etc:* The LEA may, with agreement, base its assessment on the income of the trading year ending in the last financial year before the start of the course.

2 *Anticipated income decline:* If income in the current financial year is reasonably anticipated to be 85 per cent or less of the previous year's income, then the LEA may base the assessment on the current year's income. Naturally, any such assessment will be provisional.

3 *Death of a parent:* In such unfortunate circumstances, if income has been reduced (there is no stipulation as to the amount of the reduction), the LEA may make its assessment on the current year's income. Naturally any such assessment will be provisional.

4 *Other changes of financial circumstances:* If income falls, for reasons out of the control of those being assessed, and the fall is by at least 15 per cent, the assessment may be based on the average of the previous and current year's income. Naturally any such assessment will be provisional.

There will be other miscellaneous points to bear in mind:

1 *Divorced parents:* The assessment is generally made on the income of the parent with whom the student lives.

In the event of the parents' marriage ending during the course, the assessment will be on the combined parental income up until the divorce. Afterwards, it is generally based on the income of the partner with whom the student lives.

2 *Death of a parent during the course:* The grant is immediately reassessed on the income of the surviving partner.

3 *Step-parent:* A step-parent's income is not taken into account for the assessment.

Calculating the residual income

It is the parents' total gross income that is assessed, ie before the deduction of income tax, national insurance or superannuation. Reference to the grant application form will indicate sources for some of the information. For example, those with income from employment must submit either form CS/A/M4 (Employer's Certificate) or a P60 when returning the grant application form. Although net interest payments are requested, these will be 'grossed up' (eg assuming basic rate tax is 25 pence in the pound, net interest of £75 will be 'grossed up' to £100). With dividends from company shares, the tax credit will be added to the net payment received.

Aggregate the gross income from *all* sources and then add 'expense allowances', eg car benefit and private medical insurance (referred to in the Inland Revenue as expenses and benefits in kind).

It is worth noting that certain trust income for the benefit, maintenance or education of the student is deemed to be the parents' income. However, this does not apply to scholarship payments awarded to the student by a parent's employer.

To obtain the residual income, certain allowances are deducted from the gross income. The 1989-90 allowances are:

- *Dependent adult:* An amount of £1380 for each adult dependent less income during the academic year. A dependent adult is *not* a spouse or the award holder.
- *Interest payments:* This is only allowed in situations

where tax relief is normally given. For example, interest on a mortgage for the purchase of the parents' main residence but subject to the statutory maximum (1989-90, an advance of £30,000).

- *Pensions:* Gross premiums for pension schemes to the extent that the premiums qualify for tax relief.
- *Superannuation:* Gross superannuation payments which qualify for tax relief.
- *Life assurance:* An allowance is only made if the policy was taken out *before* 11 March 1984, providing the premiums qualify for tax relief. The allowance is half the gross premium.
- *Domestic assistance:* When one parent is incapacitated, up to £1090 of the cost of domestic assistance is allowed.
- *Overseas residence:* If the parents reside overseas in a country where the cost of living is higher than that in the UK, the LEA *may* make an extra allowance.

Once having calculated the residual income, the parental contribution can be approximated by referring to Table 6, parental contribution scale. This scale is only used in connection with students entering further education since September 1988.

Parents with more than one dependent offspring will have their parental contribution reduced for the second and subsequent dependent children. The 1989-90 allowance is:

- £100 for each dependent child.

Examples of working out the parental contribution
In the examples below it is assumed that all the courses are of the standard 30 weeks 3 days duration.

Situation 1. Assume Mr and Mrs A, who live in the provinces, have one daughter who is going to a London university and that the A's residual income is £15,000. The calculation is as follows:

TABLE 6
PARENTAL CONTRIBUTION SCALE

For students first entering higher education from the beginning of the academic year 1988-89

Residual Income £	Contribution £	Residual Income £	Contribution £
10000	0	26000	2463
10600	45	27000	2651
11000	88	28000	2838
12000	195	29000	3026
13000	302	30000	3213
13500	356	31000	3401
14000	431	32000	3588
15000	581	33000	3776
16000	731	34000	3963
17000	881	34064	3975
18000	1031	35000	4151
19000	1181	36000	4338
19800	1301	37000	4526
20000	1338	38000	4713
21000	1526	39000	4901
22000	1713	40000	5088
23000	1901	41000	5276
24000	2088	41130	5300
25000	2276		

1 Points at which the scale changes: from £10600 to £13500, £1 in £9.30; from £13501 to £19800, £1 in £6.60; from £19801 upwards £1 in £5.30.

2 The contribution payable may be less than the amounts shown on the scale, particularly at the top end and where the contribution is in respect of one award holder only. This will depend on the amount of the grant against which contribution is offset by allowances for other dependent children.

3 *Note:* On 15 March 1988 the Government announced that tax relief on new non-charitable covenants would cease. The effect of this measure was to wipe out a most tax-efficient way for parents to make their contribution. To compensate, a new and more generous parental contribution scale was announced. This is the scale above. The parental contributions for students who started the course before the 1988-89 academic year are one-third higher.

	£
Maximum maintenance grant	2650
Less parental contribution	581
LEA pays	2069

Situation 2. Assume Mr and Mrs B live in London and have a son and daughter. The son is still at school and the daughter has a place at a provincial university. Assume that the B's residual income is £17000:

	£
Maximum maintenance grant	2155
Less parental contribution[1]	781
LEA pays	1374

[1] *£881 as per the scale less the £100 allowance figure for their son.*

Situation 3. Assume that Mr and Mrs C live in the provinces. They have a son and daughter, both of whom will be attending university at a town some 100 miles away. Assume that the C's residual income is £14000:

	Daughter	Son
	£	£
Maximum maintenance grant	2155	2155
Less parental contribution	331[1]	NIL
LEA pays	1824	2155

[1] *£431 as per the scale less the £100 allowance (1988-89 figure) for their son.*

The LEA would combine the two grants and pay the daughter and the son £1989.50 each:

$$\frac{£1824 + £2155}{2}$$

Situation 4. Assume that Mr and Mrs D live in the provinces and have a son who will be attending a London college and a daughter who started a course at a provincial university in their home town last year. The daughter lives at home. Assume the D's residual income is £25000:

	Daughter £	Son £
Maximum maintenance grant	1710	2650
Less parental contribution	1710[1]	466[2]
LEA pays	NIL	2184

[1] *The parental contribution as per the scale is £2276. There is an allowance of £100 for the son. The actual parental contribution is £2176. Only £1710 of this figure will be utilised for the daughter.*
[2] *The portion not utilised by the daughter (£2176-£1710).*

The sum payable by the LEA would be divided equally between the son and daughter.

The students' means test
Maintenance grants are not only assessed on parents' income but also on students. However, there are certain exemptions – both partial and full. The most important one is income from employment. The exempted income for 1989-90 will include:

- all employment income;
- scholarship income or payments from sponsoring employers up to £2750;
- the first £565 of any income (eg interest received, dividends, etc. Net interest will be 'grossed up'). Should the income from a scholarship etc exceed the £2750, the unutilised portion of this allowance can be offset against the excess;
- the parental contribution;
- attendance and mobility allowances together with any mobility supplement;

- certain trust income of dependent students *may* be treated as the parents' income. LEA's will advise.

A student's maintenance grant will be reduced pound for pound should any of the above allowances be exceeded.

Students' means test is based on income during the academic year and not the previous financial year's.

Married students

TABLE 7
SPOUSE'S CONTRIBUTION SCALE

For the academic year 1989-90

Residual Income £	Contribution £	Residual Income £	Contribution £
8400	10	21000	2298
9000	95	22000	2548
10000	238	23000	2798
11000	381	24000	3048
12000	524	25000	3298
13000	667	26000	3548
13500*	738	27000	3798
14000	838	28000	4048
15000	1038	29000	4298
16000	1238	30000	4548
17000	1438	31000	4798
18000	1638	32000	5048
19000	1838	33000	5298
19800*	1998	33008	5300
20000	2048		*maximum*

* Points at which the scale changes: £1 in £7 to £13500, £1 in £5 to £19800, then £1 in £4.

The spouse's residual income is calculated in exactly the same way as the parents' residual income – see page 36.

Married students will have their grants means-tested on their spouses' income, providing they can be termed as being of independent status. Those who are not of independent status will have their grants assessed on their parents' income. The contribution scale for the spouses' of independent students differs slightly from the parental scale (see Table 7).

If the marriage of an independent student ends in separation during the course, the spouse's means test applies only during the period of the marriage. Similarly, in situations where an independent student's marriage takes place during a course, the spouse's income is means-tested from the date of the marriage.

Applying for a grant

Introduction

The application procedure differs slightly from region to region. However, wherever you reside, it is important to apply sooner rather than later. Although theoretically applications can be held back until the end of the first term, the necessary forms should be acquired and studied as early as possible. Initially these forms appear very daunting. As most of the information you will be required to divulge generally relates to the last financial year (ie 6 April 1988 to 5 April 1989) in most cases their completion will not be possible until the new tax year (ie after 6 April 1989 to 5 April 1990).

It is extremely important that the utmost care is taken when completing the forms. Not only could an error reduce the amount of the grant awarded, but it could also result in criminal proceedings. For example, the following 'warning' appears on the application forms of one London borough:

You are reminded that you are asked to complete this form for the purpose of determining whether you or the person on whose behalf you are acting is entitled to financial benefit or advantage under the Education Acts 1944 to 1980. All information given must therefore be, to the best of your knowledge, accurate. Under section 16(1) of the Theft Act 1968, a person who by any deception, dishonestly obtains for himself/herself, or another, any pecuniary advantage, shall on conviction or indictment be liable to imprisonment for a term not exeeding five years. NB *Parents includes adoptive parents. Step parents' income is not taken into account.*

The information requested is very detailed. However, confidentiality is strictly observed. Should a parent not co-operate in filling in the forms, no maintenance grant will be forthcoming, although students in this situation may well have their tuition fees paid by the relevant LEA. All tuition fees are paid direct by LEAS to educational establishments. Students, as well as parents, must divulge their income. Parents will be required to submit evidence of income and allowances: for example, a Notice of Assessment for tax if they are self-employed; an employer's certificate or P60 for the employed; a statement or advice regarding interest received; statements or income tax assessments for mortgage interest paid, etc.

Although the appearance of the forms and procedure details may vary slightly from one authority to another, there are generally three forms that have to be completed.

Form I: establishes entitlement to a mandatory award.
Form II: determines the level of maintenance award payable. Thus, details of parents' (or spouse's income for an independent student) and the student's own income, together with details of the parents' (spouse's) mortgage interest and other dependents etc will be required. required.
Form III: this form relates to the official acceptance to the course. It should be completed and returned to the relevant LEA as soon as an acceptable unconditional offer is received, or if an acceptable conditional offer is received, when the examination results (assuming they are acceptable) have been received.

Photocopies of the completed forms should be retained for reference. Moreover, if the length of the course is not certain (eg there is an option to extend the period of study), students should apply for the longer period. This ensures that the maintenance grant will be forthcoming for the entire duration of the course should the option be taken. Take this course of action even if the option is not planned at the present moment in time.

Finally, students should note that signing a grant application binds them:

- to repay any sum paid in excess of the grant entitlement; (This also means that should a student 'drop out' of a course, a certain proportion of the award paid may be recoverable.)
- to advise of changes in circumstances.

England and Wales

Apply to the LEA within your area where you are 'ordinarily resident' on the last day of June, October or February nearest to the date on which your course starts. Should there be any doubt as to where you will be 'ordinarily resident', simultaneously apply to the likely LEAS, enclosing a covering letter.

Northern Ireland

Apply to your local Educational and Library Board for mandatory awards; discretionary awards are the responsibility of the Department of Education. See the *Addresses of Useful Contacts* on pages 165-166. The scale of awards, the means test, parental contributions etc are exactly the same as for England and Wales.

Scotland

The scale of awards, the difference in travelling costs, and allowances have all been dealt with on page 31. The means tests, parental contributions etc are otherwise exactly the same as for England and Wales. Application for a grant has to be made to the Awards Branch of the Scottish Education Department – for the address see page 165.

Publications

The Department of Education and Science publishes each year a booklet entitled *Grants to Students a Brief Guide*. This booklet relates to England and Wales, and copies are free of charge. The Scottish Education Department publishes its own booklet *A Guide to Students' Allowances:* again, this is an annual publication and copies are free of charge.

The NUS publishes a *Discretionary Award Survey* each year which outlines individual LEAS' policies to discretionary grants. A library copy should be consulted. Copies are available from the NUS at £7.50.

It is not only old age pensioners who receive an age allowance. However, a student does not have to be a senior citizen in order to qualify.

CHAPTER 4

The Parental Contribution

'The fundamental defect of fathers is that they want their children to be a credit to them.'

Bertrand Russell

THE HOUSE OF COMMONS' first report from the Education and Arts Committee Session 1986-87 was devoted to student awards. It does not make very comforting reading.

> *We are satisfied by the evidence we have received that an appreciable degree of hardship is being experienced by many students, and the families who support them, and that all students are having a great deal more difficulty in making ends meet than their counterparts a decade or two ago. The students that are worst affected are those who receive little or no parental support, but many other students too, are in difficult circumstances, including those who attend Central London institutions.*

This chapter is written for both students and parents. It is important for both to realise the potential problems faced by each other.

When still at school, most aspiring students do not give a thought to the cost of undertaking further education. Their priority is to obtain the necessary qualifications for university entrance. Each year thousands of school-leavers go on to courses of further education and there would appear to be no financial barriers. On the other hand, parents are probably very much aware that there are financial implications for them, but the extent of their possible commitment is not known. In Chapter 3 the grant system was outlined. At this stage parents can gauge approximately what their possible contributions will be.

Interestingly, although a dependent student's maintenance grant (ie the sum received for living expenses) is based on his or her parents' income, parents are not compelled to pay any contribution. In other words, if the parents' income is such that no maintenance grant, or a partial maintenance grant is forthcoming from the LEA, the parents are not forced to pay anything for the support of their offspring should they not want to do so. What is more, students in this situation will not receive an *ex-gratia* payment from their LEA. Because of the level of their parents' income, approximately 90000 students receive no maintenance grant and are therefore entirely dependent on their parents' support. The NUS estimated in 1982-83 that 43.7 per cent of parents fail to pay part or any part of their children's contributions. Should parents not complete application forms for grants, then no maintenance will be forthcoming although the individual student may have his or her tuition fees paid by the LEA. As outlined in the previous chapter, the Government's intention is to reduce the contribution to student maintenance over a period of time. However, in the foreseeable future, the parental contribution will remain.

It is acknowledged that contributions can be a burden for most parents. On the other hand, not to receive any payment from parents can be catastrophic for students. It is hoped that readers of these pages will pay or receive support. Regrettably, there is nothing that can be done if this is not the case. The problem is not so great for students who receive a grant approaching the maximum. Funds earned during vacations can go a long way to compensate for no financial support from parents in such circumstances.

So far the book has only touched upon one side of the student's budget – resources. The following chapters deal with the cost of living while undertaking a course of further education. With regional differences in prices, particularly with accommodation, it is not possible to say that a student will require a fixed amount of money each term for living expenses. However, the book points readers in the right direction so that with a little research, an individual student's living costs can be estimated with a reasonable degree of accuracy.

The meeting of minds

Students and their parents should discuss the financial implications of a course in further education. The earlier this is done the better. Parents should state what they are able to contribute and when. The student should give thought as to how much is ideally required for living expenses. It makes sound sense for the student to try to secure a vacation job and to save some money for use during the term. It is far better to be able to draw on savings rather than to finish the first term in debt. If by any chance the funds are not required, then at least savings are available if need be for foreign travel or some other project.

It is also reasonable to assume that parents are going to be more impressed if students are not only seen to be giving thought to their future, but also appear to be doing something about it. Parents and students who work together as a team and who recognise that there are problems on both sides, are far more likely to survive in harmony over a three-year period than those who completely ignore the difficulties faced by the other party. There has to be give and take as well as understanding on both sides in a student-parent relationship.

Financial help for parents

In brief, there is no financial help available for parents. However, some advice can be offered to parents who are willing to help their offspring but who are temporarily short of funds. Much is written about student finance but few appear to appreciate that parents also face cash flow crises. Parents who are quite willing to contribute towards their offsprings' living expenses at university/ college may find with the best will in the world they cannot find the required cash when it is needed. It is an established fact that the highest proportion of students living expenses and expenditure on books has to be paid at the beginning of term. Accommodation is the biggest single item. University and college authorities will require those students who are living in institutions' accommodation to pay a term's rent in advance. Land-lords in the private sector not only want a term's rent in advance but may also require a deposit.

The higher the parental contribution, the greater the pressure on parents at the start of term. Let us take an extreme example. Suppose a student going to study at a provincial university receives no maintenance grant. The LEA will advise that the annual parental contribution is £2090 a year or £696.66 a term. Ignoring the fact that part of this sum is to support the student over the Christmas and Easter vacations, the parents will be expected to pay about £70 per week (the assumption is made that each term is 10 weeks, ie £696.66 divided by 10). Most salaried parents are paid monthly and there-fore pay their contributions monthly. Therefore, on the basis of a 31-day month, it would be reasonable to expect to pay £310 for each month's contribution if a course begins on 1 October:

$$\frac{31}{7} \times £70 = £309.99$$

However, the student's estimated expenditure would look something like this in the first month:

EXAMPLE 1
ESTIMATED EXPENDITURE FOR OCTOBER

	£
Accommodation	*230*
Books	*100*
Society memberships	*20*
Food	*60*
Other expenditure (stationery, entertainment, bus fares etc.)	*50*
	460

There would therefore be a shortfall of £150 (£460–£310).

The attitude that 'all will work out in the end' could be adopted and that the student will have to finance any shortfall until the next parental contribution is made. However, the student would not be solvent until 1 December. While students can borrow at preferential interest rates (generally 1 per cent over bank base rate – certain banks also may include an element of an 'interest-free' overdraft), they are far more likely to cope with finances run from day one on a credit as opposed to a debit basis. In the previous example, the parents may decide to pay £460 on 1 October and to reduce subsequent contributions to take account of the up-front payment in October.

However, £460 may not be to hand. So what is the best way of financing any shortfall?

A loan

This may be the immediate reaction to solve the situation. However, it could result in the payment of more interest than is necessary. Admittedly the repayments can be spread over a period of time, but there is every chance that you will be able to repay the loan sooner rather than later. In other words, a facility is required that avoids the rigid formality of a conventional loan. When funds are to hand, borrowings can be reduced so as to save interest charges.

There is also every possibility that funds will be required at the beginning of each term. A flexible arrangement is therefore needed to save the bother of requesting funds on each occasion.

An overdraft

Certainly an overdraft has flexibility. However, before adopting this course of action, it is important to ascertain what the costs are likely to be. Certainly the interest rate on an 'arranged' overdraft is competitive. However, there could be other costs. For example, an administration fee may be levied for establishing the facility. This could be £10 or so every three months; the charge varies from bank to bank. Also it is imperative to check that free banking is not lost. For example, when an account is overdrawn, there could be a charge for each cheque, standing order or direct debit drawn on the account, or a fixed fee each month the account is overdrawn. Investigate the full costs of an overdraft. In fact, it may not be the cheapest form of borrowing.

A revolving credit account

This is nothing more than a packaged overdraft. Most of the High Street banks offer a branded revolving credit account. For example, there is Barclays' Cashplan, Lloyds' Cashflow and Midland's FlexiLoan. The advantage of these is that the borrowing is from a separate account and not by way of an overdraft on the main current account. The two advantages to this approach are:

1 The borrowing does not become mixed up with normal household expenditure.
2 It could well preserve free current account banking.

The latter is an important consideration. While some banks may have a monthly or annual charge for their revolving credit account facility and also possibly an item charge for each cheque issued, the costs involved are normally less than arranging a couple of overdraft facilities during the year. There are differences between the various banks' schemes. Normally the customer chooses to transfer a set sum each month to the revolving credit account and may borrow up to thirty times the monthly transfer or a limit is set on the account and the monthly transfers represent a fraction of the amount which can be borrowed. The basic principles are therefore very much the same.

Although the interest rates charged by the banks for revolving credit accounts tend to be in a fairly narrow band, the additional charges vary considerably. Annual charges range from no charge up to £35 and over.

The secured revolving credit account

The main difference between this type of account and revolving credit accounts is that the secured account is secured on the borrower's home. In other words, there is a first or second mortgage over the property. As bankers regard secured lending a lower risk, this method of borrowing has the advantage of a lower interest rate. It would be reasonable to expect the rate to be about one-third lower, for example, 16 per cent as opposed to 23 per cent.

There are relatively few of these schemes. Most of those that are available charge an arrangement fee or there are costs involved with taking the legal charge over the property. At the time of writing only Midland's Home Owner Reserve costs nothing to arrange.

It is acknowledged that the parental contribution can be a burden for' parents.

CHAPTER 5

The

Initial

Preparations

*'The only menace
is inertia.'*

St John Perse

THIS CHAPTER is not about preparing for the academic side of further education, but relates to other aspects of your new life. For example, it is far better to start the term with some cash of your own than to have no savings.

Although vacation jobs are now not as plentiful, some hints are given as to how to secure one. It also outlines such matters as tax and National Insurance Contributions.

During the weeks leading up to the start of your course, you should give some serious thought to your budget during term-time. This chapter explains how you can estimate your likely living costs at university or college. Accommodation, the possibility of a part-time job during term and an important aspect that is so easy to overlook – the insurance of your personal possessions – are also covered.

Vacation jobs

The earlier you start to look for a summer job, the better. One of the best ways of finding a job is to use the 'bush telegraph'. Let as many people as possible know that you are looking out for employment during the summer. Your parents can also put the word out to friends.

Write to local companies giving the dates that you will be available and your preference (if any) for a particular kind of work. However, within reason, you should not be too fussy. After all, the main object is to earn some money as opposed to gaining some specific work experience. Attach a copy of your *curriculum vitae* which should detail any previous employment as well as your academic achievements. It is best to keep the letter short and if possible to address it to the appropriate official by name. To find this information telephone the company and ask the receptionist. Obviously scan the local newspapers, and watch out for any notices in shop windows. Also call in at your local Job Centre.

There is always the possibility of becoming self-employed; particularly so if you have a particular skill or talent. For example, dress-making, painting and decorating, or, if a pianist or guitar player, providing live music at a local hotel or restaurant. On the other hand, it could be providing lawn-mowing, window-cleaning or car-cleaning services. The possibilities are endless. However, it has to be stressed that while the rewards can be high, it is also possible that the venture may never get off the ground. However, it is worth considering if employment cannot be found. Do not attempt to undertake work which is beyond your capability as that could be disastrous.

It is also possible to consider working away from home, for example, at an hotel on the coast. If accommodation is provided, this would be well worthwhile. However, avoid situations where all your hard earned money has to be spent on your living costs. A useful book to read on this subject is *Summer Jobs in Britain*. If your local library does not have a copy, the volume is obtainable from: Vacation Work Publications of 9 Park End Street, Oxford OX1 1HJ.

If you do find a suitable vacation job, there is always the possibility of returning for a short spell during the Christmas and Easter vacations and even the following summer. Do put the money you earn to work. Interest bearing accounts are covered in Chapter 6.

Taxation

Although your earnings from employment will not affect the level of your grant, you will be subject to tax. The good news is that tax is only paid when a certain level of income is reached. During the 1989–90 tax year, which runs from 6 April 1989 to 5 April 1990, the allowance for a single person is £2785. The allowance is revised in the budget each year.

Your grant and any scholarships or research awards you may receive are not subject to tax and therefore are not taken into account when calculating your taxable earnings. Unearned income is also subject to tax, but as is explained in Chapter 6, most savings accounts pay interest net of basic rate tax. In other words, the Inland Revenue has already been paid its dues. You may therefore only have a further liability to tax on un-earned income if your total taxable income is over £20,700 (1989-90), ie you pay tax at above the basic rate. This is unlikely to affect the majority of students. Certain social security payments, such as unemploy-ment benefit and in some cases, supplementary benefit, are taxable.

If you calculate that it is unlikely that your taxable income will exceed your personal allowance once you have commenced employment, advise your employer *before* you start work. In order that your wages can be paid gross, without the deduction of tax, you will have to sign an Inland Revenue form, P38(S). Most larger employers may have a supply to hand. If not, you can always obtain a copy from your local tax office. Signing this form does not mean that you are exempt from income tax, it merely allows your employer to pay your wages gross. Should your annual taxable income exceed your personal allowance, you will have to pay tax on the excess. If at a later date it transpires that you are likely to be in this position, advise your employer or seek advice from your local tax office.

The wheels of administration can sometimes move more slowly than you would wish. If your P38(S) is not processed before your first wage is paid, do not be unduly worried as any tax deducted will be refunded in a subsequent wage packet. Should you encounter any problems, initially consult your employer. Should the problem persist, contact your local tax office.

When you leave a job, you will be handed a 'leaving certificate' known as a P45. Keep this safely as you will have to hand it to a subsequent employer. Basically it details your income and tax paid to date. Advise your next employer if you consider that your taxable income for the tax year will be below your personal allowance.

Should you embark upon any form of self-employment you will also be subject to tax if your income exceeds your personal allowance. However, you will be able to offset the expenses of running your business against your total receipts. Consult your local tax office for guidance.

National Insurance Contributions

Your employer will deduct National Insurance Contributions from your wages – see table 8. If you take the self-employment route, obtain the relevant leaflet from your local branch of the DSS giving details of the contribution payable.

Financial planning – estimating expenditure

Although this subject is dealt with in depth in Chapter 7, before you can begin to plan financially, you must have some idea of your likely expenditure during term-time. There is no average figure that can be used.

TABLE 8
NATIONAL INSURANCE CONTRIBUTIONS

Class 1 Contracted-out rates – up to 4 October 1989

Contributions levied on weekly earnings	Employee	
	Up to £43	Excess
	%	%
£42.99	5	3
£74.99	7	5
£114.99	9	7
£164.99	9	7
£325.00	£23.61 pw maximum	

Class 1 Contracted-in – up until 4 October 1989

Contributions levied on weekly earnings exceeding	Employee
	%
£42.99	5
£74.99	7
£114.99	9
£164.99	9
£325.00	£29.25 p.w. max

Class 1 Contracted-in – as from 5 October 1989

Weekly earnings	Contracted-in	Contracted-out
Below £43	Nil	Nil
£43 to £325	2% on earnings up to £43 plus 9% on earnings between £43-£325	2% on earnings up to £43 plus 7% on earnings between £43-£325
£325+	2% on £43 plus 9% on £282	2% on £43 plus 7% on £282

Other Classes

Class 2 (Self-employed) earnings over £2350 pa	£4.25 per week
Class 3 (Voluntary)	£4.15 per week
Class 4 (Self-employed, Profits Related) Profits between £5050 and £16900 pa	6.3 per cent

These tables were prepared in March 1989 and are subject to amendment if changes are made to the Finance Bill before enactment.

Apart from individual spending habits being different (for example, a vegetarian is likely to spend less on food than a person who eats meat), the cost of accommodation varies considerably nationwide. This section shows you how to estimate your own cost of living.

Accommodation
Your expenditure on a roof over your head will be the largest single item of expenditure during the term. The NUS states in its *Accommodation Costs Survey 1988*,

'The average cost to a student in a hall of accommodation including food works out at 77 per cent of their term-time grant (the term-time grant is the full grant less the elements for travel and short vacations).' The NUS's survey gives the average weekly hall fees on a self-catering basis as follows:

TABLE 9
AVERAGE HALL FEES – SELF-CATERING 1987–88

	Cost per week
	£
London	
Universities	*27.00*
Polytechnics	*22.91*
PSHE colleges	*25.53*
Elsewhere	
Universities	*19.64*
Polytechnics	*19.77*
PSHE colleges	*20.61*

Note: *Source:* NUS *Accommodation Costs Survey 1988*
PSHE = Public Sector Higher Education

Average figures can be misleading. Accommodation costs do vary considerably on a regional basis, particularly where the private rented sector is concerned. In table 10 the costs of institutional and private sector accommodation at 21 locations are given. The data has been extracted from the NUS's *Accommodation Costs Survey 1988* and presents a reasonable cross-section. The survey is available from the NUS at £7. The 1989 edition will be ready in August, price £7.50.

Although the survey is the ideal source for obtaining the likely cost of a roof over your head, you can also do your own research. Contact your prospective university/ college accommodation office or local union and ask the cost of accommodation in hall, rented or B & B locally. Information can also be obtained regarding the policy

TABLE 10
ACCOMMODATION COSTS

	Hall Fees Weekly Equivalent Part-board[1]	Self-catering	Average Weekly Lodgings	Private Sector Costs Rented Accommodation
	£	£	£	£
LONDON				
Kings College	50.89	29.46	55.00	38.00
Queen Mary College	44.16	27.20	N/A	N/A
University College	36.08	21.51	45.00-50.00	36.00-38.00
ELSEWHERE				
Aston University	30.00	15.73	30.00	20.00
Bath University	—	18.39	25.00	22.00-23.00
Bradford University	30.89	18.90	35.00	16.00
Brighton Polytechnic	35.23	22.61	40.00	30.00
Cambridge University (Hughes Hall)	35.20	—	20.00-24.00 (b&b)	30.00-35.00
Coventry Polytechnic	37.00	24.00	20.00	38.00
East Anglia University	19.85[2]	19.92	N/A	N/A
Exeter University	—	16.12	50.00	25.00

	Hall Fees Weekly Equivalent Part-board	Self-catering	Average Weekly Lodgings	Private Sector Rented Accommodation Costs
	£	£	£	£
Elsewhere continued				
Hull University	32.16	15.10	N/A	12.00
Kent University	29.08	23.84	25.00	21.00
Leicester University	38.22	17.05	N/A	17.00
Liverpool University	36.40	19.07	N/A	20.00
Manchester University	38.75	17.81	38.00	22.00
Nottingham University	35.12	12.31	38.00	20.00
Oxford University (Lincoln College)	35.79	21.50	33.00 (b&b)	27.00
St Andrew's University	35.21	14.66	21.00	22.50
Southampton University	32.39	17.73	34.00	22.00
Sussex University	—	19.55	40.00	30.00
York University	21.63[2]	16.21	N/A	23.50

1 Part board generally comprises 7 breakfasts, 2 lunches and 7 dinners.

2 Breakfast only.

See notes page 64.

Notes to table 10, pages 62, 63.

The data has been extracted from *Accommodation Costs Survey 1988* published by the National Union of Students. The information was collected through the completion of a questionnaire by college accommodation officers and other college staff. The NUS has, wherever possible, verified all unlikely figures, but clearly cannot take responsibility for any inaccurate data supplied.

Annual hall fees are based on heated accommodation in single rooms. Part board generally comprises 7 breakfasts and dinners with lunch at the weekend.

Regional costs:

The cost of living regionally varies considerably. This is no less so for students. There is a distinct North-South divide which can result in hardship for those who study in the South-East. Whereas students in London receive additional weighting in their maintenance grants, those who live in other 'high cost' areas do not. It is not suggested that the cost of living in a particular area should be the overriding concern when choosing an institution at which to study, but it is worth bearing in mind. Our table highlights the varying cost of accommodation throughout the country.

---

for allocating rooms in hall – eg whether freshers have first preference and what your chances are of securing such accommodation.

Cost of living

The best way of discovering your likely expenditure is to talk to those who are currently undertaking a course. It would be useful if a group of last year's sixth formers could be invited back to your school for an informal chat. Failing this, contact your own friends, or friends of friends, currently at university or college. You will also be able to obtain a good idea of the cost of food by talking to your parents or checking prices at the local supermarket. It is important not to forget the 'hidden extras' of the basic cost of living, toothpaste, soap, detergent, etc, the provision of which at home you take completely for granted.

Entertainment

The money spent socialising varies from one individual to another. You will have some idea of your current level of expenditure. The sum you can afford to spend on entertainment will depend on the amount of money you have after the necessities of life have been purchased.

Books

Chapter 9 warns students to adopt initially a cautious approach to buying books and recommends buying secondhand where possible. Before the term begins, it is likely that you will be sent reading lists from your faculty or department. Generally, essential text books are indicated. Although you will not know the exact sum you are likely to spend until early in the term, at least you will be able to make a reasonable estimate from the reading lists.

Transport

The cost of travel between your home and university or college can be found out by telephoning your local bus or train station. However, there are a couple of ways of reducing the cost.

Young persons railcard
This is available to all people aged from 16 to 24 and for full-time students of any age. All you need is an application form, two passport-sized photographs and proof of age or students status, eg your registration card. Railcards cost £15. For your money you obtain:

One-third discounts on Savers – these tickets are available for most journeys over 50 miles and you can return at any time within a month – ideal for a vacation-time trip home.

One-third discount on cheap day return – perfect for a trip into the nearest main town or a day visiting friends.

One-third off standard singles, standard returns and rail rover tickets.

There is a minimum fare before 10 am on weekdays (£6 on standard returns and £3 on other tickets). However, there is no minimum fare in July and August, or Bank Holidays or at weekends. When you buy a Young Persons Railcard, you will receive a voucher which gives you a £12 discount on an inter-rail card (for European travel).

Application forms are available from your local BR station.

Students coach card

This costs £4.25 and is available to all full-time students. It discounts one-third off most National Express and Scottish Citylink standard fares. There are additional discounts on some Green Line, Oxford, Citylink, Alder Valley and M and D Invictaway services.

Application forms are available from the coach reservations office at your local bus station.

Accommodation

About 180000 students in further education, which is about 35 per cent of the total, live in university/college halls of residence. Accommodation varies from historic quarters under Oxford's spires to characterless tower blocks and even disused military bases. The amenities offered vary considerably. Some are on a self-catering basis, whereas others offer full or part board (generally breakfast and dinner every day, with lunches provided in addition at the weekend). Very often halls of residence are intended primarily for first year and visiting overseas students. Freshers who are allocated a place in hall have no problems regarding accommodation – they simply show up at the start of term and move in. However, to quote the NUS's *Welfare Manual 1988/9* regarding halls of residence:

> *Most have two things in common however – high rents and an institutionalised atmosphere – often accompanied by various restrictions and regulations.*
>
> *Thus many students either have to, or choose to, find alternatives to college accommodation. Many prefer to live in the local community, freed from institutional restrictions while many others have to find somewhere else to live whatever their preferences are.*

Whether out of necessity, or choice, you decide to live in private sector accommodation, you will need to find somewhere suitable to live. As there is a great deal of competition, the earlier you begin to look, the better are your chances of success. Here are some ideas as to where to start.

Accommodation office: This should be your first port of call, providing, of course, that your university/college offers this amenity. Most provide lists of vetted accommodation – bedsits, shared houses or lodgings.

The 'bush telegraph': A great deal of student accommodation changes hands on an informal grapevine. Freshers are disadvantaged as they are new arrivals and do not have any contacts and in any event, most of the accommodation changes hands in this way by the end of the summer term. However, it can be useful to ask college staff if they know of anything available.

Newspapers: Most local newspapers have advertisements for accommodation. Buy one as soon as possible after it is published as the competition to secure what is available will be fierce.

Notice boards: Most colleges or unions have notice boards, which among other things, feature accommodation.

Shop windows: It is always worthwhile scanning the cards in shop windows to see if there is anything suitable.

Accommodation agencies: This is an expensive source of

accommodation as tenants are charged for the services of the agency, which is generally one or two weeks' rent. In addition there could be a 'substantial' deposit and payment of rent in advance. It is worth noting that it is unlawful for an agency to demand or accept money for registering someone or for supplying a list of addresses. Pay fee only when accommodation is secured.

Many students opt for shared accommodation. Life in an isolated bedsit can be lonely. While there are obvious advantages in having a room in a shared house, there are also disadvantages. You have to get on with your fellow sharers for it to work therefore a certain degree of tolerance is required. During the course of your first year, you may make new friends and decide to share accommodation with them in your second year.

If contemplating accommodation in the private sector, a visit to your new locality two to three weeks before the beginning of term will be beneficial.

Points to note

When you do find suitable accommodation do not enter into a period of unthinking elation. Rented accommodation can be a minefield and tenancy law is particularly complex. In a book such as this, the subject can only be briefly covered. If you experience difficulties regarding rented accommodation always seek expert advice. Initially ask your local NUS, college welfare officer or Citizens Advice Bureau.

From the beginning, you will need to know your position under the Rent Act or Housing Act. You will have to ascertain if you are entering the arrangement as a licensee or a tenant. The NUS's *Welfare Manual 1988/9* explains:

> *Licences are a very controversial area of the Law and the distinction between a licence and a tenancy is often far from clear; many so-called licenses are in fact tenancies and will be treated as such by a court. The distinction is of prime importance because tenants enjoy more rights than licensees.*

Tenants

- *The Housing Act 1988 allows landlords to let on the basis of 'assured' tenure, and the related 'assured shorthold' tenure.*
- *Assured tenancies can be periodic (such as weekly or monthly), or fixed term (the Act does not specify a minimum or maximum term).*
- *To evict a periodic tenant a landlord will first have to give the tenant a written Notice of Proceedings for Possession (NOPP), on a prescribed form. It will have to state the details of the claim, as well as the ground(s) for possession. It is not a Notice to Quit (a procedure not usable under the assured and assured shorthold system). The court order, not the NOPP ends the tenancy.*
- *To evict the tenant when a fixed-term assured tenancy comes to an end the landlord has to serve a NOPP and satisfy the court that there is a ground for possession. The landlord can also serve a NOPP during the fixed-term tenancy if he or she alleges that the tenant has breached the contract.*
- *Assured shortholders are fixed term lets (six months minimum no maximum).*

  An assured shorthold tenancy is an assured tenancy subject to certain rules, the main one being that the landlord can get possession at the end of a fixed-term. Assured shorthold tenants do not have security of tenure. To evict the tenant at the end of a shorthold (or during it if the landlord alleges that the tenant has breached the contract) the landlord can go to the county court. The court must make a possession order, as long as the tenant has been given two months written NOPP at some time during the fixed term. No grounds for possession are needed other than that it is a shorthold.

(This section has been adapted from Shelter's Guide to the Housing Act 1988.)

Note: The above does not apply to contracts entered before 15 January 1989.

Licensees

- *Licensees do not have the right to Rent Act or Housing Act 1988 protection, although they may have restricted protection. They therefore usually pay whatever rent the landlord wants. In a situation of acute housing shortage, the growth of licence agreements has forced rents up very high indeed.*
- *Licenses have therefore, for obvious reasons, become extremely popular with landlords. They have become the most common method of Rent Act evasion.*
- *However, due to a ruling in the House of Lords in 1975, the majority of students will find that although they may well have signed 'licence' agreements they in fact are tenants. This dramatically improves their position as they will fall within the provisions of the Rent Act.*

A written agreement is rarely a better safeguard than a verbal one. It is essential not to sign any document before you read it – seek advice from your local NUS, welfare office or Citizens Advice Bureau if there is anything you do not understand. If you are sharing the accommodation with others, it is best to ensure that everyone is named in the agreement or rent book or that each has individual agreements. If the landlord is a resident on the premises, ascertain which parts of the property are 'out of bounds' and which amenities you may use – eg a washing machine, garden etc. Check to see whether there are any restrictions, for example receiving visitors, putting posters up on the walls, etc. If there are any defects, for example broken furniture or dampness etc, ask the landlord if he intends to put matters right. It is appreciated that if accommodation is scarce, you will be tempted not to ask too many questions for fear of losing what you are being offered. However, it is recommended that you raise as many of the issues mentioned here politely but firmly.

Obviously, you will have to discuss the rent payable. You will need to know to whom it is payable and when. If you pay weekly, the landlord must provide a rent book. If you pay monthly or quarterly, it is recommended that you give a cheque as opposed to cash. Always keep a note of when and how much you paid.

Deposits: The landlord is entitled to ask for a deposit of up to two months rent. Normally a month's rent is asked for as a deposit. Always obtain a signed receipt which clearly states that the monies represent a deposit for a specific amount. At the end of your tenancy, this should be returned in full providing no rent is owing and there has been no damage to the property.

Other charges: Ascertain whether or not you are responsible for the payment of general rates and water rates. While the rent could well be inclusive of these dues, it is essential to be clear from the outset. For students in Scotland, poll tax is applicable.

Inventory of contents: If the accommodation is furnished, you should agree an inventory of contents with the landlord. This should list all the furniture, fittings and equipment. Make a note of any damaged items found and those which are not in good condition. You will be responsible for any subsequent damage caused. Check that you are not responsible for insuring the furniture. Normally you will require cover for your own possessions. This subject is discussed later in the chapter.

Repairs: Generally the landlord is responsible for maintaining the property and certain fittings (general services such as water, electricity, etc) in good repair. Always advise the landlord if there are any problems. Should you not get satisfaction, consult your local council's Environmental Health Department.

Eviction: All tenants, and most student licensees, will be 'residential occupiers'.

As soon as you receive a NOPP seek advice *immediately* from your local NUS, college welfare office or Citizens Advice Bureau. It is an offence for a residential occupier to be 'persuaded' to leave his or her home due to harassment (eg cutting off electricity supplies, verbal abuse, denying friends access, etc). Seek legal advice if you find yourself in this unfortunate position.

To summarise the key areas to watch out for:
- Rent should not be paid before moving into the accommodation.
- On no account, whatever the problem you face vis à vis the property, stop paying the rent.
- It is important to remember that the landlord/tenant relationship is often a personal one, so normal courtesy and consideration needs to be adopted. Whenever possible, it is best to discuss things with the landlord if problems arise.

Most landlords are reasonable people. Many situations have occurred where an excellent rapport has developed between landlords and their student tenants with dinners and wine evenings being the order of the day.

Incidentally, the word landlord has been used as it has a precise legal meaning which is well established in everyday usage.

Term-time employment

Just because you are a full-time student, does not mean that you cannot undertake a part-time job during the term. Many students have a job while studying. For some a job is essential for financial survival, whereas for others it gives the means to follow a special pursuit, save for an expedition overseas or to lead a lifestyle that is above mere existence.

Income from employment will not affect your grant, although as outlined earlier in this chapter, there are possible taxation and National Insurance Contribution implications. However, these should not deter you from term-time employment. Naturally, you should not undertake a commitment which is likely to be detrimental to your academic work. As with all things, it is necessary to strike an acceptable balance. It is unlikely that an evening or two working behind a bar, or stacking shelves in a local supermarket, or even a job on Saturdays, will harm your studies. As a guide, you should not commit yourself to more than six to eight hours a week part-time employment. Note that certain institutions have strict guidelines regarding the number of hours students are able to work in paid employment. Those rules are for your protection and are not an unnecessary regulation.

As suitable term-time employment is in short supply, and as there is no shortage of takers, it is the early birds who will have the first, and best, pickings. Those wishing to be successful in the term-time job stakes *must* arrive well before the beginning of term so as to try to secure the best part-time job available.

Plan a few days stay in your new locality a week or two before fresher's week. Possibly you can combine sorting out accommodation with finding term-time employment. In any event, a spot of local reconnoitering cannot fail but to be beneficial.

Insurance of possessions

This is so easy to forget, yet it is so important. While at home your possessions would most likely have been insured under your family's household cover. It is worth checking the policy to see if this cover extends to your term-time address. While this is possible, in all likelihood it does not and you will therefore be required to make alternative arrangements.

It is false economy not to take out insurance. The incidence of theft is rising nationwide and the student community is not immune from burglary or petty pilfering. Indeed, to quote a comment made by Endsleigh, the insurance company which specialises in student insurance and which is associated with the nus. 'The incidence of theft, particularly from break-ins to student digs and other types of rented accommodation has now reached epidemic proportions.' Most of the claims Endsleigh receive are for burglary. In certain locations, the high risk areas, one in five of Endsleigh's insured students made a claim.

Sit down and work out what it would cost for you to

replace your worldly goods, ie your clothes, music centre, books, jewellery, records, cassettes and the like. It could well be in the £2000-£2500 range. To have your possessions stolen is distressing, not being in a position to replace them is even more distressing. It is not being suggested that insurance is the answer to all your problems. You will still have to take care of your possessions and be security conscious. Rest assured, the emotional experience of having an unknown individual pawing over what is personal to you and walking off with what takes his or her fancy is not pleasant.

Insurance cover is available from three basic sources:

- A specialist insurance company, ie Endsleigh.
- From a specialist insurance broker. Harrison Beaumont has been offering cover to students since 1952.
- Most of the banks include an insurance item as part of their general student package.

The cost of premiums and the cover offered varies from year to year, so there is little point in analysing previous years' offerings. However, our research over the past five years indicates that Endsleigh has the cheapest premiums if you live in a hall of residence. There is an increasing tendency for insurers to charge those who live in a high risk area a higher premium; Endsleigh has adopted this course. Consequently, its cover in private accommodation may be higher in certain high risk areas than an insurance package offered by a bank which does not differentiate between cover in a hall of residence and private accommodation and has no regional loading for high risk areas. On the other hand, a bank package can be expensive if your accommodation is in a hall of residence in a low risk area. You will have to do your own research and find a policy which is best value for your individual circumstances. Note, however, that most banks' packages are only available to their customers.

Three categories of cover are on offer. It is important to realise the difference between the covers. They are listed in rising order of cost:

Basic: In the event of an insured loss (or damage) from (in) your home, replacement is on the basis of renewal cost less an element for 'wear and tear'.

New for Old: As above, but there is no allowance for 'wear and tear'.

All Risk: Covers loss (or damage) anywhere in the UK (eg at college) and possibly in certain geographic regions abroad.

As to what cover you take out depends on your personal circumstances and what you can afford.

The various insurance schemes are not just restricted to your possessions. Included can be cover for personal accident or personal and occupier's liability under common law. All of the policies have exclusions and limitations. It is essential to choose a policy that suits your requirements.

In many cases the standard insured limit for any one item is restricted to a certain figure. This can possibly be increased if an additional premium is paid. This is an important point for those with expensive computer equipment, hi-fi or musical instruments. Our research indicates that Endsleigh is the most flexible of the insurers.

Whichever insurance policy you take out, there are some important points to remember:

1 It is *essential* to insure for the full replacement value. If you do not, any claim could be reduced by the percentage you are under-insured.
2 Avoid 'cheap' premiums offered by virtually unknown companies with the word 'student' in their title. It is prudent to deal only with established names.
3 Ensure that the cover meets your needs. It sounds obvious, but do not insure your contents for a self-contained bedsit when in fact you have a room in a shared house.

The only menace is inertia.

CHAPTER 6

Student
Banking

'Cheques aren't money.'

Andy Warhol

To attempt to survive a course of further education without a cheque account would result in too many inconveniences. A cheque book has long been considered an essential part of student life. It may not be the first time that new entrants to the world of further education have had a reasonable sum of money, but for most it will be the first occasion that the responsibility for paying for all their needs will be encountered. Daily living expenses to one side, there will be major items of expenditure such as rent or hall fees which do not readily lend themselves to cash payments. Apart from considerations of convenience there are also security aspects. Should a cheque book be mislaid or stolen, all is not lost. However, should the same happen to a wad of banknotes, the chances are that the money will never be seen again.

Banks have recognised for some time that the students of today will more than likely be good customers in the future. Consequently, all offer packages to those embarking upon a university or college course with the hope that not only will they secure the business of a high proportion of the year's intake to higher education, but it will be retained after graduation. Therefore, the packages do not necessarily cease when the courses finish, and may also include financial assistance to ease the transition from academic institution to workplace.

It must be borne in mind that financial hardship does not necessarily cease when student life is over. The initial few weeks of a first job can also be a strain on the bank account. A new wardrobe may be required or advance rental paid on a flat before receipt of the first salary cheque.

So anxious are the banks to gain a good share of the student market that their marketing promotions appear to begin earlier each year. Immediately the final examinations are over, the advertising campaigns begin in the press, on TV and radio, and by direct mail. Adults, regardless of whether they have children or not, are sent leaflets with their bank statements suggesting that it is passed to a son, daughter, relative or friend who is considering further education. As soon as course places are confirmed, branches of banks near universities, colleges and polytechnics begin to mail new entrants direct. The names and addresses of new students are provided by the nearby educational establishment. Details of the banks' student packages with offers of credit cards, overdraft facilities, cash gifts and free offers are mailed out. However, do not be totally influenced by all the non-banking incentives, for if you decide to bank with the wrong institution, it could cost you more than the free offers or cash gifts are worth in bank charges alone before the end of the first term.

This chapter examines all the points you should take into account when considering which financial institution will gain your custom. Such things as earning interest on your money – an important factor, especially if you have a pre-course vacation job – and why interest may be payable even when your current account has not dipped into the red. All the intricacies of a current account are explained in full; the text advises on what to do if you lose your cheque book, cheque card or credit card; it suggests safeguards to protect your money and examines ways of taking spending power abroad.

Savings accounts

It is a good thing to start your course with some money to hand. If possible, try to obtain a job in the summer before starting further education and save some money for use during term-time. Existing on a full grant is not easy, particularly if the cost of your accommodation is high. Therefore to have a reserve, however small, upon which to draw cannot fail but to be useful. It makes sound sense to put your hard-earned money to work, in other words, to place it into an interest-bearing account. It is unlikely that you will earn a fortune, but, as one financier once commented, 'Compound interest is the eighth Wonder of the World'. Even a modest average balance during a year can earn sufficient interest to purchase a book or to pay for an evening out.

There are a host of 'safe' places for your money. Building societies and banks have many suitable accounts for savings. The choice is yours. There are several factors, however, to take into account.

Features of savings accounts

Building societies and banks frequently launch new savings packages. The various accounts on offer may include one or more of the following features:

Minimum balance

Some institutions offer a good rate of interest providing the sum maintained in the account does not fall below a certain figure. Should the balance fall below the minimum requirement, the 'penalty' interest rate paid could be far from competitive. The suitability of such accounts depends on your individual circumstances.

Notice accounts

Some accounts require depositors to give notice of withdrawals. Generally, the longer the period of notice, the higher the rate of interest. Should you require funds in a hurry, an account with a lengthy period of notice will not be a suitable home for your savings. The banks' standard deposit accounts normally have a seven-day notice period. However, instead of requiring notice to be given, the banks deduct seven days' interest on the money withdrawn. Other accounts have a similar facility, or a penalty fee has to be paid, whilst some institutions insist that customers adhere strictly to the period of notice.

Fixed term accounts
These are not ideally suited to students as money cannot be withdrawn until the end of the contracted term of deposit, which may be a year or more. Moreover, the minimum deposit required is generally high.

Stepped interest
In recent years bank accounts have appeared that pay a rate of interest according to the size of the balance. For example, a balance up to £100 may pay 5 per cent. Once the deposit exceeds this figure 5.5 per cent on the whole balance may be paid and with sums over £500 an even higher rate may be paid on the entire balance. A variation to this is a 'banded' interest approach. For example, 5 per cent may be payable up to £100, on the next £400, 5.5 per cent may be payable etc.

Access by cash card
Some banks and building societies offer savings accounts which allow customers to make withdrawals from a cash machine with a cash card. Customers are issued with a secret number (PIN), see page 98 for general security advice.

Interest rates
Income from savings accounts is expressed as an annual interest rate. Interest may be paid monthly, quarterly, half yearly or annually. Generally, the higher the interest rate, the better it is for the customer, providing

the features of the account are suitable for their individual requirements.

Interest rates vary in line with market conditions. Rates fixed for a specific period are available, but these are generally restricted to high value term deposits. The rates you will encounter are as follows:

1 *X per cent gross* – the rate paid where interest is fully liable to income tax.
2 *X per cent net* – the rate paid after allowing for the discharge of liability to basic rate income tax.
3 *X per cent net gross equivalent* – is the rate equivalent to the net rate grossed up to take account of the discharge of liability to basic rate tax.
4 *X per cent compounded annual rate* – is the equivalent to a 'gross', 'net', or 'gross equivalent' rate annualised to take account of the compounding of interest paid other than once a year.

It is rates 2 and 4 that are the most significant. All advertisements quote the net rate and those that pay interest at intervals throughout the year sometimes quote the net compounded annual rate.

Tax and interest

Building societies have to pay interest net of tax. UK banks are also obliged to pay interest net to individuals resident in the UK. Therefore all students with accounts at these institutions in England, Scotland, Wales and Northern Ireland will always have their interest paid without liabiity to basic rate tax. The greater majority of students are not taxpayers but unfortunately the tax cannot be reclaimed. Consequently most students pay tax unnecessarily. This is unfortunate, but regrettably unavoidable.

Although it is possible to obtain interest gross from certain sources, there are disadvantages. For example, banks in Jersey, Guernsey and the Isle of Man pay interest without the deduction of tax but they are not very accessible. Some National Savings products pay interest gross, but to obtain a good return it will be necessary to place your funds in a product that either requires one or three months' written notice of withdrawal. Although a National Savings' ordinary account has instant access, the gross interest on sums below £500 is generally less than the net rates obtainable from commercial institutions. Added to this is the fact that interest is only earned on whole pounds deposited for a calendar month and no interest is payable on sums deposited or withdrawn during a month. Although up to £100 can be obtained at any post office (including sub-offices) on production of the pass book, in circumstances where more than £50 is withdrawn the passbook has to be sent to the National Savings Bank for checking. Consequently, there are periods when account holders will be without withdrawal facilities. This can prove to be most inconvenient.

Suitable homes for savings

Last year, Lloyds and Midland Banks started to pay interest on students' current accounts. It is now anticipated that it will not be long before all banks pay interest on current accounts; indeed, some banks and building societies have already introduced interest bearing cheque accounts. However, prior to actually starting your course, there may be other accounts offered by building societies and banks which give a better return than current accounts. Do research to see what is on offer.

Before deciding where to earn interest on your savings, take note not only of the account features outlined above but also consider the convenience of the institution's location before opening an account. In other words, you do not want to travel a considerable distance in order to withdraw or deposit money.

When you begin your course it makes sense financially to keep money not immediately required in an interest-paying account. Should the bank you choose not pay interest on current accounts, it is well worth considering opening some form of savings account with the same institution or a building society. If your money is split between two institutions, do think of the inconvenience factor. Above all, do not have funds in a savings account when there is the possibility that your current account is about to become overdrawn. Quite simply, even at preferential interest rates, the cost of an overdraft is more than the interest earned on a savings account.

There are two interesting points to note. If you deposit a cheque into a building society account, the sum it represents begins to attract interest the next day. However, with a bank, sums represented by a cheque generally do not begin to earn interest until the third day after it has been paid into the account.

Nevertheless, there is one important difference between building societies and banks which could be very important to you. Currently, if you pay a cheque into a building society, the funds it represents cannot normally be withdrawn until seven working days have elapsed, unless other arrangements were made at the time of deposit. Banks are far more tolerant. They generally allow you to withdraw funds represented by a cheque on the third day after it has been paid into a savings account. Their rules are slightly different with regard to current accounts – see Bankers' Clearing System on page 101.

Banking in the future

At the beginning of 1987, the Government gave building societies additional powers which permitted them to compete more with banks. Consequently, societies are not just a provider of mortgages for home purchase and a suitable home for savings, they now offer cheque accounts and can lend for other purposes. However, to date, none of the societies have launched an account specially for students. Possibly this will alter in the future. Keep an eye out for developments. Societies will one day wish to attract students as current account customers.

Whereas building societies have become, or are becoming more like banks, the latter institutions have been encroaching upon the societies' preserves. It was not so long ago that the interest rates offered by banks were not competitive with the returns savers could obtain from building societies. This is no longer the case. Banks now compete favourably with building societies. What is more, banks are now a significant presence and very active in the mortgage market. Up until the end of the 1970s, banks left finance for home purchase to the societies. Both now compete for this business. The result is that it is no longer necessary to establish an account relationship with a building society so as to receive preferential treatment for a mortgage at some future time.

As societies do not as yet offer packages orientated towards students, our analysis of banking is consequently restricted to banks.

Cheque accounts

Which bank?
When the banks first began to cater specifically for the student incentives were offered ranging from a plastic folder and biro to a map of the city where their university or college was situated. How things have changed!

Each year new incentive packages are launched which are intended to be more pleasing than their predecessors. At the time of going to press the banks still have their 1989 student accounts under wraps.

As the packages change each year watch out for press advertisements and displays in local branches throughout the summer. Collect as many of the leaflets outlining the offers as you can. Perhaps a cash gift or a free present may appeal. However, you should look not only at the 'freebies' but also the banking terms of each package.

Banking terms
The two most important banking aspects of a package are:

1 Free banking;
2 An overdraft facility at preferential rates.

We now point you in the direction of what to look for when analysing the offers. All of the packages offer both free banking and overdrafts at preferential rates, but there are finer points which you must appreciate in order for your analysis to be worthwhile.

Free banking

First it would be useful to examine what 'free banking' actually means. Just as there is no such thing as a free lunch, there is also no such thing as free banking. What it does mean is that the customer can operate the current account without charge. In other words, providing certain conditions are met, all cheques, cash machine withdrawals, standing orders and direct debits payments from and all credits to the account are without charge. Interest will naturally be charged on the money you borrow. In addition, you will have to pay for certain services. For example, if you stop a cheque, or want a statement to replace one you have lost or wish to send money abroad etc. It is only reasonable to pay for such extras and normally you will be advised of the cost when you avail yourself of a particular service.

The above paragraph stated that free banking was subject to certain conditions. For the public at large this may mean that the account must be kept in credit or within an agreed overdraft limit. Charges may be made on the basis of the activity on the account, for example 30 pence for each cheque, or there may be a fixed fee for the charging period. In addition, an administration fee is normally charged for an overdraft. In brief, it could mean a quarterly charge of up to £30 or on occasions it could be more.

Banks have always had a different approach for students. Although the conditions for free banking differ from one institution to another, there have only been three basic approaches in the past:

Case 1: The account is maintained in credit or within an agreed unspecified overdraft limit.

Case 2: The account is maintained in credit or within an agreed specific pre-determined overdraft limit, eg up to £200.

Case 3: There are no stipulations as to the size of overdraft or as to whether it is agreed.

Initially the different criteria all appear to be harmless. After all, there have to be some rules for determining whether an account is operated free and it is only reasonable that banks adopt different strategies. However, there is a potential danger in the Case 2 situation. In our example, those students who arrange an overdraft for £210, will lose the privilege of free banking, in other words they could find themselves paying £30 or more a term to operate their account.

These situations are called 'charge traps': although thankfully they are becoming a rare species. Possibly the banks have taken note. Chapter 8 deals in greater depth with them and advises how they can be avoided. However, examine the various leaflets to see if you can spot any still available in 1989. They can take the following guises:

Maintain your account in credit and we will operate it free of charge.

What does this mean? Simply, there will be no fees for cheques, cash machine withdrawals, standing orders, direct debits, statements or credits.

This is even the case if you take advantage of our £250 overdraft offer. Naturally, we will charge you interest on the money you borrow, but running the account will not cost you anything.

Should you overdraw your account by more than £250, you will incur additional bank charges on your account during the charging period.

Regardless of the balance on your account, we will run it entirely free. There will be no quarterly commission charges for cheques, statements, standing orders, cash dispenser transactions, direct debits or credits. Should you take advantage of our free £100 overdraft facility, your banking still remains free.

In the first example, free banking will be lost if an overdraft of over £250 is arranged. In the second example, free banking is lost with overdrafts over £100. Do not avoid a bank just because you spot a 'charge trap', but turn to Chapter 8 and follow our advice to avoid it being sprung.

Overdraft at preferential rates

All of the banks include some form of special overdraft deal in their packages. However, the various offers do vary. For example, you may find:

1 All agreed overdrafts are at a 'preferential' rate.
2 All agreed overdrafts below a certain sum are at a preferential rate.
3 There may be a free overdraft up to a certain sum either for any purpose or only in certain circumstances (eg a delayed grant cheque).

Interest rates are examined in some depth in Chapter 8. However, we will briefly mention one or two points here. 'Preferential' generally means 1 per cent over the bank's base rate. This is a good deal and is at least two-thirds below the rate paid by the public at large (who incidentally may also have to pay an administration fee when an overdraft facility is made available).

'Agreed' means that you have to ask the bank for an overdraft and it agrees the amount and term of the facility with you. It does not mean you agree to borrow from the bank. Guidance is given as to how to ask for an overdraft in Chapter 8. There are a few tips which cannot fail to impress your bank manager.

Branch location

In addition to the various offers and banking terms, thought must also be given as to where you are going to open your account. There is no use in deciding to use a particular bank if you have to travel miles to its nearest branch. There are three basic possibilities, although for students living on campus this is reduced to two, namely points 1 and 3:

1 In your parents' home town.
2 Close to your term-time accommodation.
3 Near to your university/college.

Most students prefer the last option as it is a convenient choice. There is also the added advantage that branches near to further education establishments are more student orientated. They tend to understand the problems that can be encountered and have specially trained 'student advisers' at these branches. The three options will now be examined in turn.

Parents' home town

Perhaps you already have an account at a branch local to your home. If you have been satisfied with the service you have received then there is no reason to transfer your account to a branch in the city or town where you will be studying. Retaining your account at 'home base' also has the added advantage that you are a known individual as opposed to just another account. When you become a student, you will be entitled to the student package, including the free gifts. Do not forget to advise the branch of your new status, so not only can you claim your free gifts but also to ensure that your general banking terms are switched from the ordinary personal tariff to the student package.

There is one point to bear in mind if contemplating 'arms-length' banking. With a cash card it is possible to obtain cash from cash machines to which your bank is linked. For example, Midland, Nat West, and the TSB have a reciprocal arrangement whereby customers of one bank can use their own bank's machines and those of the other two. With a cheque book and cheque card you can cash a cheque at any branch of your own bank without incurring any additional charge. However, other banks generally charge non-customers a fee for cashing cheques (which must be supported by a cheque card) *unless* they are located on a campus site. So, if there is no bank or a convenient branch of your own or handy cash machine on campus, cashing a cheque elsewhere could cost you £1 on each occasion. Your branch should be able to advise you of the nearest bank's representation to your place of study should you not have any local knowledge.

If you do decide on 'arms-length' banking, arrange an 'in-case-of-need' overdraft before you depart for your course. This will save any panic should your grant cheque be delayed or you have any other need for funds in an emergency. Always liaise with your branch before exceeding the agreed limit and obtain consent to an increase in your overdraft facility.

Close to term accommodation
This may be convenient for certain students. However, remember that you are likely to spend more time at university/college while banks are open than at your term accommodation.

Near to university/college
This is most convenient during the term but is not handy during the vacation. However, you will be most likely to need your branch close by during the term. For this reason, most students prefer this option.

How to open an account

Although there are a few simple formalities to complete, opening a bank account does not take long. If possible, you should not leave opening an account until the start of the term, for not only could you find yourself in a long queue with others in the same position as yourself, but it will delay the issue of your cheque card as these are prepared at a central location. A cheque book without a cheque card is not very useful as most shops, garages and restaurants do not accept cheques which are not guaranteed in this way.

Opening an account in person
Simply go along to the branch where you wish to open the account. Have the following, if available, to hand.

1 Some form of identification which may take the form of a passport, driving licence etc.

2 The letter from your local LEA advising that it will pay your fees, noting whether or not a maitenance grant will be forthcoming. This letter is evidence that you are a *bona fide* student eligible for the bank's student package. The free offers and cheque card are generally not forthcoming until this has been seen by your bunk.

3 The letter advising that you have been accepted for your course. (This may not be required by all banks.)

If the last two items are not yet available, do not delay opening an account for this reason. You may have to present the letter from your LEA later. However, the bank can at least order your cheque card and issue you with a cheque book.

Opening an account by post

Most banks with branches near further education establishments recognise that students may not wish to leave their banking arrangements until the last minute. Opening an account by post also allows the bank's staff to order cheque cards, cheque books, etc so that all is available for students to collect at the beginning of term.

There is no need to make a special journey to set the formalities in motion. More than likely you will receive a letter from all the bank branches near to your university/college. Not only will a leaflet be included which outlines each bank's student package, but an account opening form will be included. Providing you complete and forward the form in good time (say, two to three weeks before term begins), your cheque book, cheque card, gifts etc will be waiting for you at the start of the academic year. When you call to collect them, have to hand:

1 Some form of identification.
2 The letter from your LEA.

Transferring an account between branches

If you already have a bank account in your home town and wish to transfer it to the bank's branch nearest your university/college, contact your branch. You will either be given guidance as to what to do or the necessary arrangements will be made on your behalf. Do not forget to claim your free gifts. The letter from your LEA will be required (see previous page).

It is strongly advised that the transfer is not left until the last minute. This will hopefully safeguard you against being in a transitional state at the start of term with one account having been closed but the other one not as yet opened. Ask your old branch if you can retain your cheque book and cheque card until you have been issued with replacements by your new branch.

Transferring an account between banks

This is possible, but it is a lengthy procedure. Simply close your account at one bank and open it at the other institution. However, should you prefer to transfer your account, please note that the branch of your new bank and not your old one should be asked to make the arrangements.

Operating a cheque account

Maintaining records

Cash has an in-built warning system that advises us when it needs replenishing. You know when your spending power is becoming low as your wallet looks decidedly thin and your pocket or purse no longer contains high value coins. On the other hand, as far as the account holder is concerned, a cheque account has no instant early warning system to advise that all is not well. Rest assured, your bank manager will be well aware of the situation. Admittedly, you will receive regular statements and you can obtain a balance of your account not only from your branch, but also from cash machines. There are also facilities which show a print-out detailing the transactions on your account since your last statement. Nevertheless, statements and balances can never reveal a completely up-to-date picture of your account and they cannot project into the future. You may have written cheques that are still in the system or a credit paid in at another branch may not have yet reached your account.

It is possible to have an early warning system that will advise you if you are about to run out of funds. If you inadvertently dip into the red your overdraft will not be an agreed one and there is every possibility that you may therefore not qualify for free banking. With very little effort such expensive mishaps can be avoided. You should try to keep an up-to-date running record of your account. All that is required is a simple note of your account transactions. Start with the balance, add on payments into the account and deduct payments out. Do not forget to make a note of withdrawals from cash machines and if you make payments by standing order and direct debit these should also be deducted from your running balance at the appropriate time. It would be a good idea to keep a list of any standing orders etc so that you have a record of the dates when the various sums are payable.

Banks have two types of cheque books. The traditional ones have counterfoils which are used to record the details of the cheques issued. The newer types have pages at the front in which customers may record payments in and out of their account together with their balance. As some customers consider that such record pages are a little too public for their personal financial affairs, most banks give their customers the choice of a traditional or 'new' type of cheque book.

Those cheque books without counterfoils have the advantage of being an inch or so smaller and consequently may be more convenient. Of course, there is no need to complete the balance column of the record pages. A separate note book can be used for maintaining your current account transactions.

Whichever method you adopt, bear in mind that your records are only as good as you make them. Your early warning system will be defective if you make a mathematical error or do not record all your transactions – cash card withdrawals are common omissions. Above all, do take action if the balance diminishes to a low level. Your bankers will be far more impressed if you advise them of your impending cash flow crisis rather than them breaking the news of your liquidity problems to you. Finally, remember that if you go overdrawn without agreeing an overdraft facility, not only will you possibly lose free banking but you will also not have the advantage of borrowing at a preferential interest rate.

Details to record
Always make a note of the following when you issue a cheque:

1 Its date.
2 To whom it is payable.
3 The amount.
4 Its serial number.

Either complete the counterfoil (which has the serial number pre-printed) or the records page. Should the cheque be lost your bank will require all these details when you 'stop' the cheque (see page 110 for what to do if one of your cheques is lost).

Statements
When you receive a statement do not simply file it away but carefully check all the transactions against your own records. These may not necessarily agree with the statement, simply because a cheque you have issued has not yet been deducted from your account. Should you not be able to reconcile the two records of your financial affairs then investigation will be required. Banks are not infallible and mistakes do occur from time to time, although thankfully this does not happen often.

What to do if you find a mistake
Banks' records are very good. For example, they film the cheques and credits they send to London for clearing and either keep cheques that their customers write for several years or return them to customers with their statements. The same applies to credit vouchers. So, should there be something amiss, the matter will

normally be swiftly rectified. Should you consider that there has been a mistake with your account, contact your branch.

The receipt for the money you pay into your account is the credit slip counterfoil. They will want sight of this. The most common cause of complaint is cash machine withdrawals. It is appreciated that this is a difficult area as the customer generally cannot prove that funds were not withdrawn personally from a particular machine on a certain day. It is also very easy to forget making a withdrawal. However, if you have any problems with your bank that are not resolved to your satisfaction, you can contact the Banking Ombudsman, see Addresses of Useful Contacts at the end of the book.

Of course, not every error is detrimental. However, 'Bank Error in your favour, collect £200' is reserved for the game of Monopoly. While it may be tempting to keep quiet about your windfall, it is essential to tell your bank. So, do not rush out and buy that CD player or new outfit, but pop-in and see your branch manager. Legally you are only entitled to the money if you honestly believe that it is yours. As most students would find it difficult to convince a learned judge that they have a fairy godmother who showers riches on them from time to time, honesty is the best policy. Of course, if your bankers insist that you have an unknown and generous benefactor, that is a different matter. However, before you decide to throw a party or book a world tour by Concorde, do insist that they confirm *in writing* that the money is yours.

Cheques

There is nothing mysterious about writing a cheque. It is simply an instruction to a banker to pay money from your account. Theoretically, it is possible to write a cheque on a cow. However, it is recommended to stick to the conventional cheques as supplied by your bank – it makes life far simpler.

There are one or two rules of general security to keep in mind.

- Sign your cheque card with a ballpoint pen as soon as your receive it.
- Always keep your cheque book and cheque card in a safe place.
- Never keep your cheque book and cheque card together.
- Above all, please do not leave your cheque book and cheque card unattended in a public place, eg locked in a car or hidden among your clothes in a changing room.

Although you will not be held responsible for cheques drawn on your account with a forged signature, the loss of your cheque book and cheque card will cause you inconvenience.

Banks lose millions of pounds each year as a result of fraud following cheque book and cheque card thefts. Pages 110-113 outline actions to take if you lose your cheque book and/or cheque card.

Rules to follow when writing cheques

- The first is obvious, never sign blank cheques. If you do happen to order something by post and you are not sure of the cost make out the cheque to the company/person, write out the amount for example as, 'No More than Ten Pounds', leave the amount in figures blank and sign the cheque. Also see 'Safety Measures' below.
- Another obvious point is: Never write in pencil or erasable ink or type cheques. This is to prevent forgery.
- The amount in words should start as far to the left as possible and should be written without large spaces between the words.
- Draw a line after the amount in words so that there is no empty space.
- If writing a cheque for round pounds, draw a line after the last figure to the end of the amount box.

- Note that a bank is not liable for any losses which cannot be detected readily.
  For example, if you write a cheque for £7, and some unscrupulous individual alters it to £70 you must bear the loss if the addition of the 'ty' and the '0' in £70 is not readily apparent.

A cheque is an instruction to a bank and consequently the information it contains must be clear and precise. Banks do not like instructions that are muddled. Indeed, if there is any doubt about what a customer is telling them to do, they take a course of action that can lead to their making no mistake – they do nothing. Generally a bank will not pay a cheque if there is any doubt regarding their customer's instructions. In banking terms this is known as a 'technical irregularity'. The exception, of course, is when the amount of the cheque is within the cheque card limit and has the card number written on the back – in other words, the cheque is guaranteed. In this case the bank will pay a cheque signed by a customer regardless of the muddled instructions. Here are a few points to remember:

The date: Banks will generally not pay a cheque which is more than six months old. However, they do recognise that each January some customers will absent-mindedly date their cheques for the previous January. Cheques which are more than six months old will normally be returned marked 'out of date'. Bankers will also not pay cheques bearing a future date. The reason is simple, their customer did not intend the cheque to be paid until the date on the cheque and indeed has the right to stop the cheque before that date arrives. Such cheques will be returned marked 'post dated'.

Payee: The technical term for the person (or company) to whom the cheque is payable. Always insert the payee's name to avoid any possible dispute, for example, another party could insert their name. If a banker receives a cheque not bearing a payee's name it will be returned marked 'payee's name required'.

Amount: The amount in words must agree with the amount in figures. If this is not the case, the cheques will generally be returned marked 'words and figures differ'. Banks tend to ignore differences of a few pence and pay the lesser of the two amounts.

Signature: Try to be consistent with your style of signature for you may have problems with supporting your cheques with your cheque card. Advise your branch if there is any marked change. Unsigned cheques will be returned marked 'drawer's signature required'.

Alterations: You must sign alongside any alterations you make to a cheque. If this is not done, the cheque will be returned marked 'alteration requires drawer's confirmation'.

Cashing own cheques

There are two ways of cashing your own cheques:

1 Write 'cash' after 'pay' and fill out the cheque for the amount you want to withdraw from your account and sign it.
2 Write your name after 'pay', complete the rest of the cheque and then turn it over and sign your signature on the reverse. This is technically known as an 'endorsement'.

Most people prefer the first option as it is less laborious. Banks tend to issue their customers with 'crossed' cheques. As is explained in the Safety measures section below, this means that only the account holder can cash the cheques. Consequently, you cannot ask a friend to draw cash from your account on your behalf.

When you cash a cheque at a branch where your account is *not* maintained, you will need your cheque card. The banks allow customers to cash one cheque per day up to the guaranteed limit (currently £50). It is a condition that:

1 The cheque is signed in the cashier's presence.
2 The cheque book as well as the cheque you wish to cash and the cheque card is handed to the cashier.

The reason for both conditions is security. Signing the

cheque in the cashier's presence is obvious. The second condition will become apparent when you look at the back of your cheque book. There will be a page which resembles a calendar. When a cheque is cashed supported by a cheque card, the cashier will blank out the day of the month of encashment. It is worth remembering that there is no additional charge when cashing a cheque at any branch of your own bank. However, other banks charge non-customers a fee for cashing cheques *unless* they are located on a campus site.

Emergency encashments

You may find yourself short of cash when you are away from base. If you have your cheque card to hand and only want a sum up to the card guarantee limit, it will be just a normal transaction. Even if you do not have your cheque book and/or cheque card with you, it *may* be possible to obtain cash, providing you have adequate identification. Ask a branch of your own bank if they can help. If they can, you will have to pay an administration charge and possibly the cost of a telephone call.

Should you have your cheque book and card, but require more than £50, this may be possible upon payment of an administration fee which may or may not include the cost of the telephone call to your branch. An alternative approach, which may save you any extra charges is to cash a cheque at one bank and then proceed to another and cash a further cheque. In this situation, the second bank will not make any charge for contacting your branch when it telephones to enquire if your cheque book or card has been reported stolen. Some additional identification may be requested.

All cheques are personalised and the account details are computer readable. Consequently they must only be used by the person to whom they are issued.

Safety measures

Take a look at one of your cheques. More than likely there will be two parallel lines which extend through the area where you write the payee's name and the amount in words. Technically these are known as 'the crossings'. It is strongly recommended that you only use crossed cheques. Ask your bankers for a book of crossed cheques should your cheques not be crossed. The crossings not there for ornamentation, but are an instruction to a banker that the cheque can only be paid to a third party through a bank or building society account. Only an uncrossed or 'open' cheque can be cashed by a third party and then only at the branch of the bank on which the cheque is drawn. Even with 'open' cheques, the cashier will want some form of identity from the payee before handing over the money. Although a safeguard, identification is not foolproof. If there has been some mischief, any loss will either be borne by the account holder or the real payee. It is most unlikely that the imposter who cashed the cheque will be traced.

Thieves are reluctant to pay cheques into their own bank accounts. Banks' records are meticulously kept and the accounts to which the cheques were credited will be traced. Of course, instead of paying it into his or her own bank account, the thief may 'endorse' it, ie sign it on the back with a signature purporting to be that of the payee and pass it on to some unsuspecting third party. In such circumstances, the person who issued the cheque could be the loser. However, it is possible to obtain some protection against foul play with your cheques, just by adding a few words within the crossing. For example:

Account payee: The addition of these words is an instruction to a banker accepting the cheque into an account to only credit it to that of the named payee. Failure to follow the instruction could result in an action for negligence being brought against the bank. As bankers are extremely cautious creatures by nature, they will heed the instruction.

Not negotiable: A cheque bearing these words can be endorsed over to a third party, but he or she receives no better title than the endorser. So, if a cheque so crossed is stolen and is endorsed over to some unsuspecting person, that individual will be the loser.

It is not generally appreciated that if an account holder's cheque is stolen from the payee and is endorsed over to an unsuspecting third party, the account holder can be the loser *if* the cheque was not crossed 'not negotiable' or 'account payee'.

In all multi-occupied accommodation where there is much coming and going, mail can vanish or be lost before it is received by the addressee. As a precaution, ask your parents to cross any cheque they send you with the words 'not negotiable'.

Paying money into a cheque account

Your branch may well issue you with a book of personalised credit slips, or there may be some credit forms at the back of your cheque book. When using these there is unlikely to be any errors as all the information the bank requires to credit your account (other than the amount you are paying-in) is pre-printed.

When using 'blank' credits found in the banking hall, always ensure that you insert all of the following details:

1 The name of your bank.
2 The name of the branch at which your account is maintained.
3 The branch's 'sorting code' number. This is printed in the top right-hand corner of your cheques.
4 Your name.
5 Your account number.

There can therefore be no possibility of the credit going astray.

Always keep the counterfoil bearing the cashier's stamp or if using an 'autodeposit' machine (in which you drop a special envelope containing the cheque(s) and completed credit) keep the printed receipt as evidence of having made the deposit. Only discard your receipt when the credit appears on your statement.

When you pay a cheque into your account which is not drawn on your branch of the same bank, you will not always be able to withdraw the money it represents until the third day after your account is credited. Should you draw against the funds it represents before this period has elapsed, you will pay interest even though you are not overdrawn. Therefore it is necessary to ask your bank if you may draw against uncleared funds.

Paying in at a branch other than your own

It is not necessary to visit your own branch to pay into your account. You can credit your account via any branch of the high street banks, by simply handing your credit to the cashier. If you do not have your book of pre-printed paying-in slips with you, there will be a supply of blank ones in the banking hall.

If you do take advantage of this system, there are two points to note:

1 The credit will not reach your branch until the second working day after you made the transaction. In other words, if you paid in on a Monday, it would not reach your account until a Wednesday.
2 Branches of your own bank will not charge for this service but other banks may levy a small fee.

The bankers' clearing system

As Andy Warhol once said, 'Cheques aren't money'. How true a statement. If you receive cash you know that you have money you can spend. On the other hand, with a cheque you never know whether you have the spending power until your bank has received the cheque's money from the branch of the bank on which it is drawn. All sorts of things could go wrong. Perhaps the cheque is not paid because of lack of funds, or some technical irregularity, or because payment has been stopped by the person who issued it.

However, there is no need to be alarmed. Only a fraction of 1 per cent of the total number of cheques the banks deal with in a day are unpaid. Nevertheless, the funds represented by any cheque(s) paid into your account will not necessarily be available immediately. Until such times that your branch receives funds from the branch of the bank upon which a cheque is drawn, the money represented by the cheque is said to be 'uncleared'. Of course, not all cheques have to be cleared. A cheque which you pay into your account at your branch which is drawn on the same branch of the bank does not have to be processed through the system. Theoretically, the funds it represents are available immediately. However, such items are still subject to payment and *could* be unpaid for any of the above reasons. Ascertaining whether payment can be confirmed when cheques are paid in is a grey area.

When you pay in a cheque not drawn on your branch
It takes four working days for a cheque drawn on a branch other than the one where your account is maintained to be cleared.
The procedure that it undergoes is as follows:

Day 1:   (i) You pay the cheque over your own branch counter.
(ii) Your account is credited.
(iii) Cheques are sorted by the bank.
(iv) After the close of business the cheques are despatched to the Bankers' Clearing House in London.

Day 2:   (i) The cheques arrive at the Clearing House.
(ii) They are sorted into branch order.
(iii) Bundles of cheques are returned to the branches on which they are drawn.

Day 3:   (i) The cheques arrive at the branches on which they are drawn.
(ii) It is decided which cheques will not be paid – they are sent back by first-class mail to the branches at which they were paid in.
(iii) Those that will be paid are posted to customers' accounts.

Day 4:   (i) The unpaid cheques, the Royal Mail

permitting, arrive back at the branch where they were paid in.

(ii) The unlucky customers' accounts are debited.

(iii) A letter is sent to you advising that the cheque was not paid.

(iv) The banks settle their accounts for the aggregate value of the cheques which started their passage through the system on Day 1.

What this means to customers

The Bankers' Clearing System has very important implications for account holders. Until a cheque is cleared, the customer does not have a right to draw against the funds it represents. This means if you pay a cheque into your account at your own branch, which is drawn on another bank or another branch of your bank, you *may* not be able to draw against the funds it represents until three days afterwards.

However, should you require the funds before this period has elapsed, ask the cashier if you can draw against it when you hand over the credit. Undoubtedly the answer will be in the affirmative where a grant cheque is concerned. The only time the bank is unlikely to grant your request is when you want to draw a considerable amount against funds represented by a large cheque drawn on a private account. However, all is not lost in such a case. It is possible for the branch to 'by-pass' the clearing system by 'specially presenting' the cheque. Providing it is paid, and the Royal Mail permitting, you should be able to obtain access to the funds the next day. Nevertheless, there is a charge for this service. Ask the fee that will be payable as it varies from bank to bank and can be as high as £10.

Should your branch allow you to draw against 'uncleared funds', whether the cheque is 'specially presented' or not, interest will be charged until the cheque is 'cleared' (ie until the third day after it was paid in). So, although your statement may show that your account has never been overdrawn, you will pay interest when drawing against an 'uncleared' cheque. In normal circumstances the charge will be minimal.

If you issue a cheque to a third party against uncleared funds, your bank could return your cheque unpaid. It would be marked 'effects not cleared'. This is only likely when you are drawing a large sum against an uncleared balance. In normal circumstances the funds will have been cleared by the time your cheque reaches your account – unless you bank at the same branch as the payee.

Cash cards

Automatic Teller Machines (ATMS) or cash machines have revolutionised personal banking. No longer is it necessary to visit a bank during opening hours to obtain cash. Even when branches are open there seems to be a preference to obtain cash from a machine rather than from a cashier. Banks, bemused that their customers are prepared to queue in the rain to obtain cash from an ATM when the banking hall is empty, now install cash machines inside their branches as well as outside. Some banks even allow access to indoor machines at night. Customers can gain access to the lobby by using their cash card as a 'key'. ATMS are now no longer restricted to bank premises. They can be found at railway stations, in supermarkets and even in motorway service areas.

This is all very convenient – some may say too convenient. Modern technology may have eased access to your bank funds, but at the end of the day remember all the bank notes which appear from ATMS are indirectly from your account. Most machines issue a slip showing the time and amount of your withdrawal. Keep this as a reminder to up-date your own record of your account. It is also worth checking the sum withdrawn. The machines are manufactured to a high specification and are tested regularly. However, mistakes can happen. If you are 'short changed', overpaid, or a withdrawal appears on your statement which you did not make, refer to your branch. If matters are not resolved to your satisfaction, you can take the matter up with the Banking Ombudsman, see page 165 for addresses of useful contacts.

A cash card is becoming more than just a means of obtaining funds. They can be used to obtain balances and instant mini-statements of your account. Your bank will advise of the extra services that your card may provide. Balances and statements will only be obtainable from your own bank's machines. However, it may be possible to secure cash from other bank's ATMs. You will be told of such arrangements when you are given your card.

The operation of cash and other automatic machines is simple. You insert your card into the slot, tap in your Personal Identification Number (PIN) and follow the instructions on the screen. Up to an agreed amount of cash may be withdrawn in any one day or week. Certain machines, but not all, check your balance before dispensing the money.

Safety measures are built into the machines to prevent unauthorised use. Generally if there have been more than two attempts to activate a machine with an incorrect PIN, the card will be retained. However, such fail-safe mechanisms should not result in an air of complacency. Generally, as a cardholder, your liability with regard to unauthorised withdrawals by third parties only ceases when the bank has been informed of the loss of the card. In cases where the PIN has been revealed, the cardholder can be liable for all withdrawals. It is virtually impossible to prove that you have not revealed your PIN, therefore it is important not to reveal your PIN to anyone. If you have problems which cannot be resolved to your satisfaction, refer to the Banking Ombudsman.

General security measures
- Keep your card safe and never keep the disguised number with the card.
- Commit the PIN to memory, or if it is really necessary

to make a note of it, do not record it in a way that allows another person to discover it.

- Destroy the note from your bank advising you of your PIN immediately after memorising the number.
- Never reveal the PIN to anyone – not even bank staff. Bear in mind a favourite ploy is for the thief to ring the cardholder posing as a police officer or bank official. On some pretext that the card may have been found and that proof is required to check that it in fact belongs to the cardholder, the unknown individual will ask for the PIN. Do not fall for this ploy.

There have been some incredible acts of stupidity with cash card PINs; an individual who wrote the number on the card or the person who wrote the PIN in an address book under cash card. Both lost substantial amounts of money. As a student you will find your finances stretched enough without an unknown person siphoning funds from your account. It is bad enough losing money, but if your cash card and PIN are obtained by a third party, you could also find yourself in debt.

Recommendation: Regularly check that you still have your cash card as there is a danger period between the card going missing and the bank being advised of the loss.

Essential: Even if you have not lost your card but believe that there is a possibility that your PIN has been discovered by a third party (for example, if your mail has been intercepted), advise your branch immediately.

Care: Do not keep your cash card with any electronic security pass as this could damage the card.

If you do lose your card turn to page 110 and read the section on, What to do if cards of cheques go missing.

Credit cards

While it is not generally a prudent method of borrowing, nevertheless this form of 'plastic money' can be most useful. However, credit cards are not recommended to those who cannot control an urge to spend money. Used prudently, they are beneficial as up to 56 days free credit can be obtained. However, credit cards can also seriously damage your wealth. Moreover, they are an expensive way of borrowing money.

If you have sufficient will-power to resist going on spending sprees that you cannot afford, it makes sound sense to pay for goods, and services with a credit card as opposed to using cash or cheques. Provided you settle the account in full by a certain date (generally 25 days after the statement is issued – the exact date is clearly shown on the statement), you will incur no charges. This also means that you can continue to earn interest on the money you would have otherwise spent until you reimburse the credit card company.

It is important to keep track of your credit card expenditure and to 'earmark' the funds. Naturally the benefit of the period of free credit will be lost if you forget to settle your credit card dues on time. The credit card companies are beginning to introduce direct debit facilities whereby they automatically take the sum due from your current account on the appropriate date. However, before taking advantage of this service, do ensure that the facility is for the full amount due as opposed to the minimum payment (generally 5 per cent of the balance, minimum £5). If you only pay the minimum amount you will, of course, incur interest charges. If your card company does not offer a 'full statement' direct debit service then you must remember to pay the full amount on time. So as to avoid postal delays and the cost of a stamp, the account can be settled by taking the credit card slip which is attached to your statement, together with your cheque, to any bank displaying the credit card symbol (eg Access or Visa). No charge is made for this service. If using this method, payment must be made four working days before the latest settlement date. Failure to observe this rule will mean the period of free credit is lost even if you are only one day late.

As a useful tip, if a branch other than your own is used to settle the credit card account, there will be a further few days of grace before your cheque is deducted from your account. This is because the cheque will be in the clearing system for three days. If the credit is paid over your own branch counter, the cheque will be posted to your account on the same day.

General security measures

- Sign your card with a ball-point pen immediately you receive it.
- Do not leave the card in a locked car or hidden in clothing in a changing room. Always keep it locked away at home or safely stowed on your person.

Using a credit card for payment by telephone or post

When ordering theatre or concert tickets, payment may be accepted by telephone if you use a credit card. This is so much more convenient than sending a cheque or calling in person – provided the telephone lines are not constantly engaged! Bookings made in this way cannot be cancelled, however. The tickets may be sent out to you by post or, if the timescale is short, you may be asked to collect them from the box office on the night. Have your credit card handy if collecting the tickets in person. This is a security measure to ensure the tickets are handed to the right person.

Credit cards are also useful for mail order purchases. Advertisement coupons or order forms often have facilities for paying by credit card, so you can take advantage of the period of free credit when ordering by post.

When paying for goods or services by telephone or post, you will not have a sales voucher to remind you of your expenditure. So do not forget to up-date your own running balance of the amount you owe your credit card company.

Payment by credit card in person

Credit card companies have various safety checks to minimise their losses from fraud. Do not be embarrassed or take it as a personal slight if a retailer telephones for authorisation, even when the amount you are spending is small. It simply means that a temporary low 'floor limit' on the part of the retailer has been imposed as a matter of routine. All shops have a normal limit up to which they can accept a credit card payment without reference. This varies from one establishment to another.

Of course, If you exceed your credit limit, the transaction may not be authorised. Also, in certain cases, you may be asked to produce identification or asked for your address or date of birth (which will be checked against the credit card company's records). This is another routine safety check. For example, if a card has been used heavily in a single day, or if it is the first transaction for a considerable period, or if it is for a large amount, the credit card company is not unreasonably put on alert. Many stolen cards, the loss of which has not been noticed by cardholders, have been recovered in this way. So, should you be asked for additional identification, do not be offended.

Care should always be taken to ensure that the sales voucher is fully completed. Restaurants in particular leave the 'total' box empty so that the customer may pay the tip by credit card. Disappointed waiting staff are not unknown to award themselves a tip if the customer has not seen fit to do so.

An added protection when paying by credit card

It is not generally appreciated that consumers who pay for goods and services by credit card have an added protection. Under the Consumer Credit Act 1974 the credit card company is 'jointly and severally' liable with the supplier for any breaches of warranty where the goods or services purchased with the card cost £100 or more (but less than £30,000!). In other words, if you buy defective goods by credit card and cannot get satisfaction from the retailer, or if you pay by credit card and the supplier goes into liquidation before you receive the goods or services, you may be able to obtain reimbursement from your credit card company. If you do find yourself in this unfortunate situation, contact your credit card company. Your local Citizens Advice Bureau will be able to advise you in particular situations.

If a PIN is obtained for use with your credit card (eg for cash machine withdrawals or 'cashless' shopping experiments), the same precautions should be taken as with cash card personal numbers. Note that credit card withdrawals from a cash machine, or payment for travellers cheques or foreign currency, are 'cash advances' and either attract interest from the day the money is obtained or a handling charge. Whichever course your credit card company takes, the effect is the same for you – it costs you money.

NEVER exceed the card's credit limit. Ask for an increased line of credit if necessary. This will save you the embarrassment of having a transaction declined.

Lost your cheque book or cards?

Introduction

Students are as vulnerable as any other member of society in having their possessions stolen. Those who live in multiple occupied accommodation such as a hall of residence, or a house divided into flats, are probably at greater risk than the public at large. There are more people coming and going so that an opportunist thief can easily blend in with the general bustle. As you can never be sure if a 'visitor' is a *bona fide* guest, or an unscrupulous individual on the prowl for easy pickings, always lock doors and windows when you are out. It pays to be security conscious.

Card protection schemes

In recent years there has been a growth in the number of card protection schemes; the concept of which is very simple. You register all your cards with the company which operates the scheme. If you lose your cards, you simply ring one number and the company notifies your bank and all your credit card companies. There is an annual charge for the service.

In principle it is a good idea. Certainly in the past

some banks have either included a year's free membership or provided the service at a concessionary rate in their student packages. However, as most students have only a couple of cards, you may feel that the annual fee is not worthwhile at the moment.

Some schemes also include other features, for example, a key or baggage retrieval scheme or emergency cash if you are stranded without funds. Again, the advantages of such 'extras' depend on your own circumstances. If you are planning to travel abroad, it is probably beneficial.

If you do join such a scheme, do not forget to make a note of the procedure to follow when a mishap occurs. It is useless to participate in a card protection scheme if you do not know what to do in an emergency.

The best schemes are those that cover you for fraudulent use *before* the credit card companies have been notified, providing you advise the card protection scheme within 24-hours of your loss.

What to do when your cheque book and cheque card go missing

A cheque card should never be kept with a cheque book. In the unfortunate event of either, or both, going missing, here is what to do:

• Advise your branch immediately.
• Details of the last few cheques issued will be required, so try to recall when the cheque book was last used, and to whom the cheques were made out.

Only cheques signed by you will be deducted from your account. You will not be responsible if someone has forged your signature. A replacement cheque book and card will be issued as soon as possible. The bank may require your help if there is a police enquiry. If the cheque book and card turn up at a later date, do not use them but advise your branch straight away. Generally no charge is made when either a cheque book or cheque card is lost.

Banks lose over £20 million a year with cheque book and card fraud. Do your bit to combat crime and be careful.

What to do if one of your cheques is lost

If you or the payee loses a cheque, you should advise your branch immediately and give the following information:

- The cheque's serial number.
- The date on the cheque.
- The name of the payee.
- The amount of the cheque.

The details that will be required emphasise the need to keep a complete and accurate record of all the cheques you issue.

The missing cheque will be 'stopped' if it has not already been paid. A charge is made for this service. Should the cheque be found at a later date, it should be destroyed and your bank advised of the fact. Your branch will advise you as to what action to take if the cheque has already been paid. You should follow the same procedure if you want to stop payment of a cheque for any other reason (eg faulty goods). But remember you cannot stop a cheque guaranteed by a cheque card.

What to do when your cash card goes missing

Generally, a cardholder's liability for unauthorised withdrawals by third parties only ceases when the bank has been informed of the loss of the card. In cases where the PIN has been revealed, the cardholder can be liable for all withdrawals. It is therefore important to keep your PIN a secret.

In the event of loss, the following procedure should be followed:

- Advise your bank (via any branch) immediately the discovery of the loss is made.
- Some banks have telephone hotlines see the Addres-

ses of Useful Contacts section (page 165) if you have not made a note of the number to ring.

- As a double safety measure in case of any breakdown in communications, always advise the account holding branch in addition to using the hotline.
- The bank will want to know the date, time and place that you last used the card, so jog your memory.
- In no circumstances reveal your personal number to any person who asks for it after the card has been stolen. Bank staff or police will *not* want to know the information. There is no charge for a replacement cash card.

What to do if a credit card goes missing

- If this is noticed during banking hours, contact the branch of the bank where the current account is maintained.
- At any other time use the credit card company hotline.
- When telephoning the hotline, the credit card number will be required. This will be found on your statement or on a sales voucher.
- Details of the last transaction will be required, ie the date, amount and name of the shop, garage, etc.

The Consumer Credit Act 1974 limits your liability to £50 if the card is used fraudulently before you advise the credit card company. Once you have advised them of the loss there is no further liability. If you have never used your card (ie it was lost in the post) you are not liable for any loss if it is fraudulently used.

If you were issued with a PIN for use with your credit card, you may be held responsible for all unauthorised cash machine withdrawals. It is a condition that the PIN is kept secret. As mentioned in the Cash Card section, it is virtually impossible to prove that you have not disclosed your PIN.

Paying your way abroad

Travel may broaden the mind, but it can also be a strain

on finances. However, many students take advantage of the various travel deals available and make at least one trip abroad during their period of study. The object of this section is not to advise you on how to finance travel but to outline the various ways that you can take your hard earned spending money to foreign climes. Some banks include some form of travel deal in their student packages. For example, they may waive the commission charge for foreign currency or travellers cheques.

Foreign currency
It is not always possible in the UK to obtain currency of the country you are going to visit. For example, the Russian rouble and Moroccan dirham cannot be exported, so they are unobtainable outside their respective countries. In such situations, there are either banks at the port of entry or exchange facilities at hotels. Certain countries have restrictions on the amount of their own currency that can be taken into their country by tourists. Your bank will advise you of any restrictions at your destination.

When obtaining foreign currency, do not take all your holiday money in foreign bank notes; there are far safer ways of taking spending power abroad such as travellers cheques.

There are one or two points to bear in mind before returning home:

1 If the currency cannot be exported, you will need to convert all your foreign money into sterling before setting off for home.
2 While notes and coins from countries with no currency restrictions can be converted into sterling in the UK, the rate of exchange for coins is poor. It is not recommended to bring your foreign coinage back to the UK: either spend your surplus coins abroad or convert them into bank notes before returning home.

Travellers cheques
As the advertisements state, 'they are so much safer

than cash'. All of the major issuers of travellers cheques offer emergency assistance to customers who lose their travellers cheques. This does not mean that you can be careless. While every effort is made to assist the customer, the speed with which this can be done depends upon location as well as the other factors. However, as a safety net it is very comforting.

There is one simple proviso in the case of loss or theft. Each cheque should be signed immediately the purchase is made in the space marked, 'signature of holder'. Do not countersign the cheques until necessary.

At the time of purchase you will be given a sales advice slip. It is important that this is taken abroad with you. However, do not keep it with your travellers cheques as it outlines the procedure to follow in the event of loss and also states the unique numbers of the cheques. The advice slip should be kept with your general travel documents. Each issuer has its own procedures but generally you will have to contact a local office or telephone the company's UK base. If it is not possible to reverse the charges, all reasonable communication costs are normally reimbursed. The 'hotlines' are generally manned 24-hours a day. The details required by Thomas Cook in the event of loss are typical of other issuers of travellers cheques:

- full name and permanent address of the holder;
- brief circumstances of loss;
- currency of cheques and the value of those lost;
- serial numbers of missing cheques (so keep a note of those cashed);
- serial number of *all* cheques purchased;
- full name and address of establishment where purchased;
- date of purchase;
- holder's present contact address.

Currency and denominations

Travellers cheques are available in various currencies, including sterling. The main foreign ones are: Australian, Canadian, Hong Kong and us dollars, French and Swiss francs, German marks and Spanish pesetas. When visiting the United States, it is essential to take travellers cheques in us dollars. With 'out of the way' destinations, it is best to seek advice from your travel agent or bank.

There are obvious advantages in taking travellers cheques in the currency of the country which you are visiting. Your spending power will not be affected by fluctuating exchange rates and it may be possible to spend cheques in shops and settle restaurant and hotel bills. Change will, of course, be given in local currency. This will save encashment commission charges.

If you consider that exchange rates will move in your favour while abroad then it could be advantageous to take sterling travellers cheques. Perhaps you want to hedge your bets by taking a mixture of currencies, ie in sterling and the currency of the country being visited.

Whatever currency you choose, it is strongly recommended that you take a good proportion of small denominations in order to minimise the amount of cash you need to carry. However, do bear in mind any minimum encashment charge.

Cashing travellers cheques abroad

Cash your travellers cheques as and when you need funds; perhaps cashing amounts sufficient for your spending needs over two or three days. Banks tend to offer a better exchange rate than bureaux de change or hotels. Also enquire as to the commission you will be charged. Sometimes a good rate of exchange may be counteracted by a hefty commission fee.

Countersign the cheques in the cashier's presence. Remember to take your passport as it may be required.

Unused travellers cheques

Sterling travellers cheques can be countersigned and paid into your bank or building society account. Travellers cheques in foreign currency can be converted into sterling at your bank.

The cost

The standard fee for purchasing travellers cheques is 1 per cent of the total value of the order. Some banks waive this for students. If your bank does not, it is worthwhile enquiring if any local building societies issue travellers cheques free of commission charges to account holders.

Eurocheques

When eurocheques and eurocheque cards were launched in the UK they were called 'a financial passport to Europe'. Basically, they are a versatile form of the standard UK cheque book and cheque card. In Britain the customer writes cheques in sterling, in France in French francs and so on.

When supported by a eurocheque card, each cheque is guaranteed up to £100 or its approximate currency equivalent. Any number of eurocheques can be guaranteed in a single transaction. With the standard UK cheque card only one cheque is guaranteed per transaction.

Cost

There is an annual fee for the eurocheque card. Certain banks incorporate a free eurocheque card as part of their student package.

Cheques issued in the UK are charged at the bank's standard tariff. In other words, if you qualify for free banking, there will be no charge. When issued abroad, there is a modest fixed fee for each cheque plus a percentage charge (currently 1.6 per cent) levied on the value of the cheque. Eurocheques issued in foreign currency are converted into sterling in the UK. The exchange rates used are competitive.

Eurocheques in practice

There is no doubt that eurocheques are a great concept. Unfortunately there have been a few problems. In France, shopkeepers have been known to insist that the cheques are written in French, while banks have levied an additional encashment charge. The latter is recoverable from UK banks. Not so long ago, Moroccan banks which proudly display the 'ec' symbol, refused to cash eurocheques. However, the Moroccan situation is now improving and even shopkeepers in the depths of Marrakesh's souk now readily accept them.

You should regard eurocheques as a useful part of your finances while abroad. As the value of cheques issued is deducted from your UK current account, ensure that there are adequate funds available, whether in the form of a credit balance or an agreed overdraft facility.

Credit cards

Credit cards are more versatile than eurocheques as they are accepted internationally. It is not suggested that credit cards will enable you to pay your way in remote areas, but certainly it appears that credit cards know no geographic limits. They are used in shops and to settle hotel and restaurant bills exactly as in the UK and you will receive up to 56 days free credit. The sums spent appear on your statement in sterling. There is no evidence to suggest that the exchange rates used for the conversions are uncompetitive.

It is also possible to obtain cash, subject to local conditions, at banks displaying the appropriate credit card symbol. However, you will be charged either interest from the date the money is taken or a handling charge. Whichever method is adopted, it is not without cost to you. In an emergency, however, the charge will no doubt be worthwhile. Be careful not to exceed your limit. If you are going to be away for a long period, make arrangements for your dues to be paid in your absence.

Credit cards are a useful means of paying your way abroad and ideal in an emergency situation. However, 'plastic money' is best in the hands of the financially responsible. Those who spend impulsively are well advised to leave their card in the UK and undertake their travels without the risk of bankruptcy.

CHAPTER 7

Financial Planning

'Real richness is in how you spend your money.'

Jacques Lipchitz

IN ANY situation where resources are limited, it is essential to plan. Arranging your life is perhaps one of the most common forms of planning undertaken by man. It may be quite mundane and extremely short term, for example, deciding what to do tomorrow. Forward planning may take the form of organising activities for the weekend or a holiday. The busier your social life becomes, the greater the need for more sophisticated planning. Of course, life is not just one big social whirl. There is work to be done, perhaps meetings to attend or some essential tasks that have to be undertaken. Time is a scarce resource but its uses are infinite. Planning its optimum use requires choices to be made and compromises to be reached. In other words, a balance has to be struck between working, socialising and rest. The pressures of work may require an evening out to be cancelled.

Planning your life will come as second nature. Admittedly some people are better at it than others. When you start university/college you may have to experiment in order to achieve the correct balance between working and socialising. However, there is one aspect of planning that may be totally new to you – financial planning or budgeting. It may well be the first time that you have been responsible for making a given sum of money pay for all your needs – accommodation, food, books, socialising and a host of items ranging from laundry to toothpaste that were previously on hand without cost to yourself. Unfortunately there is not as much leeway with money as there is with time. When all the hours in the day have been utilised, another day begins. However, when money is spent, it is not automatically replenished. Whereas you can make up for lost time relatively easily, the same does not apply to cash. It is well-known that the value of grants has declined in real terms over recent years. It is therefore more difficult for students to manage financially. Planning finances is therefore even more important than in the past.

In Chapter 5 it was suggested that prior to the start of your course you researched what your living costs would be during term-time. With the information gathered you will be able to think about your finances. It was also recommended that you worked out your financial planning route before embarking on your course. Of course, expenditure is only one side of the financial equation. However, by early September you should also have a good idea of what your resources are likely to be during the term. If you have not been advised by LEA of your maintenance grant, you should be able to calculate the sum roughly (see Chapter 3). Also by this time you will know the sum your parents are prepared to contribute to your living costs and the amount of money you have been able to save during the vacation.

Mapping out your financial plan

The following is a hypothetical example to show one way of formulating a financial plan. It has to be stressed that the figures given are illustrative, giving an example of the mechanics of financial planning. Let us assume that our fictional student, Emma, will be studying in the north of England. For the first year she will be living in self-catering accommodation on campus.

Resources
Emma has estimated her resources as follows:

EXAMPLE 2

	£
Her income per year will be:	
Maintenance grant	*1500*
Contribution from parents	*630*
Savings	*400*
Her income each term will be:	
Maintenance grant	*500*
Contribution from parents	*210*
Total	*710*

Emma is fortunate as she found work during her vacation and was able to save a reasonable proportion of her earnings. Her parents will make her an allowance which is marginally above the sum advised by the LEA as being the Parental Contribution – £630 as opposed to the sum of £590 calculated according to The Education (Mandatory Awards) Regulations.

Expenditure
Emma's term is 10 weeks in duration. She estimates her expenditure as follows:

EXAMPLE 3

Estimated expenditure for term	£
Accommodation	220
Travel between home/university, including one weekend back home during term	50
Food at £15 per week	150
Miscellaneous (stationery, incidentals, toiletries, detergents etc)	30
Laundry	30
Books	100
Society memberships	20
Entertainment	100
Total	700

According to Emma's calculations, she should be able to balance her budget. However, there is no margin for additional expenditure. Clothes are missing from her budget, but she does have savings of £400 to draw from should she wish to add to her wardrobe.

Calculating the weekly estimated expenditure

Emma will, of course, have to purchase her fare to university when she departs from home. Certain payments will have to be made by her in the first week of term. Shortly after arrival, the college authority will present its account for the term's rent, books and certain stationery items will have to be purchased at the beginning of the course. Society subscriptions will be payable during the first week. Emma's immediate dues will therefore be:

EXAMPLE 4

Estimated immediate dues	£
Return fare home/university (she will take advantage of a cheap weekend return mid-term)	30
Accommodation	220
Books	100
Society memberships	20
Miscellaneous	15
Total	385

Allowing for the £20 required for the weekend home, Emma's weekly allowance will therefore be:

$$\frac{£700 - (£385 + £20)}{10} = £29.50$$

Let us break down the estimates of Emma's term expenditure on a weekly basis:

EXAMPLE 5

Estimated expenditure per week	£
Food	15
Laundry	3
Entertainment	10
Miscellaneous	3
Total	31

There is a 'shortfall' of £1.50 per week but Emma is confident that she can reduce the money she spends on food and entertainment by this amount.

If Emma only spends an average of £29.50 each week, all should be well. However, plans do not always work out according to expectations. It is important not to devise a financial plan and then forget about it. As William Feather, an American businessman, once remarked, 'A budget tells us what we can't afford, but it doesn't keep us from buying it.' Emma will have to monitor progress if any form of planning is going to be worthwhile.

Monitoring your financial plan

One of the most financially optimistic characters has to be Micawber in Charles Dickens *David Copperfield*. His finances were always shakey, nevertheless he lived in the hope that something would 'turn up'. Despite his observation about income and expenditure, practice and theory were hard for Mr Micawber to co-ordinate.

It is not suggested that a temporary cashflow problem will make you miserable. But plunging into debt and being unable to extricate yourself from the problem will not lead to happiness. Indeed, severe cases can result in worry that is detrimental both to your health and your studies. The best course is to remain in control of your finances. This is achieved by monitoring your financial plan regularly, perhaps weekly in the early stages of your study. As time progresses and your expenditure pattern becomes established, your financial judgement will become more intuitive. However, this does not mean that you can become complacent. Regular monitoring is still required but at less frequent intervals.

Monitoring sounds a grand word, but it is a simple process. The key to it is the personal early warning system for your current account. This is nothing more than your own up-to-date running record of your account. If Emma were to check that her financial plan was on course at the end of the sixth week of term, she would initially multiply her current weekly estimate by the number of weeks remaining before the vacation, which in her case would be four:

$$4 \times £29.50 = £118$$

If the balance in her account plus cash in hand was more than this figure then she would know that all appears to be well. However, she will only be on course if her expenditure is going to remain at £29.50 per week until the end of term and that no special purchases or social events are planned. Perhaps there are a couple of books she needs to buy for reading over the Christmas vacation. If she has not yet spent the sum she estimated for such purchases, she could still be on course. All she has to do is calculate the amount of unbudgeted expenditure over the last four weeks of term and check whether she has sufficient funds in her account over and above the £118 required for 'living expenses'. For example:

EXAMPLE 6

Unbudgeted expenditure	*£*
College dinner	*15*
Books	*20*
Retreat weekend	*30*
Total	*65*

It is now necessary for her to check the revised expenditure against her available resources.

EXAMPLE 7

Revised expenditure		*Available resources*	
	£		£
Weekly allowance	118	Bank	121
Unbudgeted		Cash	14
expenditure	65	Building society	350
	183		485
	Surplus £302		

Thanks to Emma's savings she does not have a cash flow crisis. However, not all students are as fortunate. Emma's situation is also unusual as her parents paid all of their contribution at the start of term.

Adjustments to a financial plan

A financial plan must never be regarded as rigid. It will have to be altered to take into account changing situations. For example, should you discover you are spending more on food each week than you expected, money spent on, say, entertainment may have to be trimmed. Naturally, expenditure will not be constant each week. As long as everything averages out in the long run, there should be no problems.

The following is another hypothetical example. Again it is stressed that the figures given illustrate an example of the mechanics of financial planning. Let us assume that our fictional student, Dave, is in exactly the same situation as Emma – his grant and parental contribution are precisely the same and his estimate of the term's expenditure. In other words he too anticipates that a weekly allowance of £29.50 will cover his day-to-day living expenses. The only difference between the two is Dave has no savings.

Suppose that Dave has spent £130 on books during

the first four weeks of term against his estimated expenditure of £100. In addition he joined the rambling club and his walking boots and protective clothing cost him £70. This expenditure was not planned. At the end of the fourth week of term, Dave has spent £575. The breakdown is as follows:

EXAMPLE 8

Actual expenditure during first four weeks of term	*£*
Return fare home	*30*
Accommodation	*220*
Books	*130*
Society membership	*15*
Boots & protective clothing	*70*
Food	*50*
Entertainment	*40*
Laundry	*5*
Miscellaneous	*15*
Total	*575*

When he monitors his financial plan, the following is revealed:

$$6 \times £29.50 = £177$$

In other words, according to his original estimated level of expenditure, he requires £177 for the remaining six weeks of term. The only problem is that Dave's resources only total £135, showing a shortfall of £42. If Dave is to remain solvent over the next six weeks, he has to revise his finances. His revised weekly resources are:

$$\frac{£135}{6} = £22.50$$

Therefore, he has either to reduce his weekly expenditure by £7 per week or to find resources of £42. Here are possible courses of action:

1 To ask his parents for an extra £50.
   This is a possibility, but:
   (i) Dave may want to be independent;
   (ii) his parents may be already 'stretched' financially;
   (iii) it could lead to friction between himself and his parents and an inquest into his lifestyle.
2 Find a part-time job.
   This would certainly be a solution, but:
   (i) suitable situations tend to be scarce after the start of term – there is a scramble for key vacancies at the beginning of the academic year;
   (ii) it is always important not to allow a part-time job to jeopardise academic work. Nevertheless, a sensible arrangement is unlikely to be detrimental.
3 To economise.
   This is a good old-fashioned 'tighten your belt' solution, but:
   (i) although the amount Dave has to cut-back is not high in absolute terms, it is nevertheless over 23 per cent of his weekly budget;
   (ii) while some economies can no doubt be made, the average student budget is usually well-trimmed to begin with.

Obviously in a financial crisis, economies must be made if possible. However, cut down on social expenditure rather than food.

As to which course of action is taken to rectify an 'over-spend' situation depends on individual circumstances. Despite all efforts, on occasions this may not be possible.

When there is a liquidity crisis

Let us suppose that Dave manages to cut his expenditure down to £25 a week for the next four weeks. His resources at the end of week 8 would be £35 (being the £135 he had at the end of week 4 less the £100 he spent over the following four weeks). Dave works out his likely expenditure until the end of term:

EXAMPLE 9

Estimated expenditure for the *last two weeks of term*	£
Food	*30*
Entertainment	*30*
College dinner	*15*
Books	*15*
Miscellaneous	*10*
Total	*100*

His expenditure and available resources makes sorry reading.

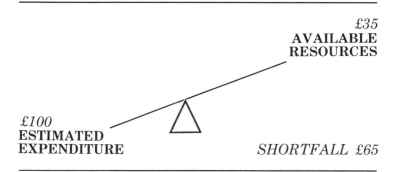

£35
**AVAILABLE
RESOURCES**

£100
**ESTIMATED
EXPENDITURE**

SHORTFALL £65

Dave is not unduly bothered as he knows that during the two weeks of the Christmas vacation he will be able to earn £200. However, he realises that he will have to finance the shortfall until he has received his wages. Moreover, although he will not be expected to pay his parents board and lodging, he will want some money during the holiday. He knows that his grandparents are going to give him £50 for Christmas and that his parents will also give him some cash, but on the other hand, he will need to purchase gifts for the family. He works out his financial plan on a weekly basis from the start of the holidays.

EXAMPLE 10

WEEK 1 OF THE HOLIDAYS

Estimated Expenditure £		*Resources* £	
Entertainment	15	*Beginning of week*	*(65)*
Miscellaneous	5		
	20	Less *expenditure*	20
		End of week	*(85)*

WEEK 2 OF THE HOLIDAYS

Estimated Expenditure £		*Resources* £	
Entertainment	25	*Beginning of week*	*(85)*
Miscellaneous	5	*Add wages*	100
Purchase of gifts	40	*New position*	15
	70	Less *expenditure*	70
		End of week	*(55)*

WEEK 3 OF THE HOLIDAYS (CHRISTMAS WEEK)

Estimated Expenditure £		*Resources £*	
Entertainment	10	*Beginning of week*	*(55)*
Miscellaneous	5		
	——	*Wages*	*100*
	15	*Expected cash gifts*	*75*
			——
			120
		Less expenditure	*15*
			——
		End of week	*105*

Note: *Bracketed figures signify an overdrawn position.*

So, by the end of Christmas week, Dave will be in a stronger financial position than he was at the start of term. However, he does have a liquidity crisis towards the end of term and for the first half of the holiday. Ignoring the possibility of a temporary family loan, Dave must approach his bank at the end of Week 8 and ask for an overdraft facility. His estimated maximum overdraft is £85 but he would be well advised to add a margin and ask for an overdraft of £120 until the start of term.

Show the bank your financial plan. A bank manager is always impressed when a customer is seen to have thought about the situation. Any margin which is above your estimated maximum overdraft may be explained as a contingency in case of any emergency need.

When overdrawn, always pay available funds into your account as soon as possible so as to reduce the interest you pay.

Financial planning is essential. It does not matter whether you do the calculations on the back of an envelope or formulate a more elaborate plan in a ledger. The most important thing is that you do something about it. And remember, your estimates should always be realistic; if not, you are wasting your time. It is essential to revise your plan when you realise that your actual expenditure varies from the sums you anticipated having to spend on specific categories.

Our own researches reveal that the majority of students budget. The exception appears to be those reading accountancy. However, ignoring the case of those who specialise in financial matters (who in our view budget intuitively), failure to keep an eye on finances is tempting disaster.

When all the hours in the day have been utilised, another day begins. However, when money is spent, it is not automatically replenished.

CHAPTER 8

Student Borrowing

*'Two of the most beautiful
words in the English language
are Cheque Enclosed.'*

Dorothy Parker

IN THE 1986-87 session of Parliament, the House of
Commons Education and Arts Committee turned its
attention to the subject of student awards. Various
organisations were asked to give evidence to the
Committee on students' finances. A spokesman for the
Committee of Vice-Chancellors and Principals advised
that, 'Students have begun to turn to the banks for
support. An informal loan system appears to operate
already, as it is commonplace for students to have
overdrafts, often running at an average of £300 to £500.'
Dr Smith, Director of Kingston Polytechnic confirmed
the need for students to borrow: 'I am sure your
Committee has heard it before, but the reality is that
the majority of students run up overdrafts. The typical
pattern is that in a term a student will run up an
overdraft of £200 and by the end of the course, as he or
she approaches graduation and the prospect of employment, £500-£1000 would be common.'

The Association of University Teachers described the
level of student hardship as 'unprecedented' since the
1960s. This is because maintenance grants have not

kept pace with inflation. In February last year, the Secretary of State for Education and Science was asked to 'indicate for each year since 1977, the value of the maximum student grant outside London, at constant 1987 prices.' The response emphasises just how much grants have declined in real terms.

TABLE 11
'ELSEWHERE' RATE OF GRANT IN 1987-88 PRICES

Academic Year	Grant £	Academic Year	Grant £
1977-78	£2271	1983-84	£2042
1978-79	£2294	1984-85	£2017
1979-80	£2230	1985-86	£1964
1980-81	£2210	1986-87	£1980
1981-82	£2130	1987-88	£1972
1982-83	£2063		

Notes:
1 Repricing is based on the RPI for September each year.
2 For the years 1977-78 to 1983-84 an adjustment has been made to take account of revised arrangements for travel expenses introduced in 1984-85.

It is therefore not surprising that students are facing hardship. Nevertheless, it is estimated that only about 50 per cent of students resort to borrowing at some stage during their course. It must also be stressed that not every student who dips into the red runs up an ever-increasing overdraft. Many who borrow during the term manage to clear their indebtedness from vacation employment. Of course, some borrowing is of a temporary nature – for example, if a grant cheque is late or if parents have delayed sending their contribution.

There are cynics who consider that students' financial difficulties are entirely of their own making. In certain cases an extravagant lifestyle could be the root of the problem. However, the majority of students are financially responsible but nevertheless incur hardship on occasions, if not at all times.

This chapter deals with how to borrow money. It does not suggest that students *must* borrow, but should they become short of money at least the cheapest ways of securing funds will be known. Whereas it is easy to borrow money, it is far more difficult to pay it back. This point should be borne in mind.

It is essential to give some thought as to why your financial affairs have deteriorated. Sometimes the reason is obvious and out of your control – a late grant cheque, for example. However, on other occasions it may be because of your own mis-management. Perhaps a riotous evening out will be recalled with regretful nostalgia or an unneccesary purchase looked upon dolefully. But, even those who manage their financial affairs cautiously can face problems from time to time.

Interest rates

Before examining the subject of borrowing, it is essential to examine briefly the costs involved. Banks are aware that students suffer cash flow crises from time to time and consequently they tend to include some form of borrowing at a preferential rate in their student packages. These vary from year to year, but it may incorporate an overdraft up to a certain sum free of charge. This could be restricted to particular circumstances, for example if a grant cheque is late, or there may be no stipulations as to why funds are required.

Most banks include an overdraft facility at a 'preferential' rate. Generally, this means 1 per cent over the bank's base rate. Base rates vary from time to time, so the cost of borrowing also fluctuates. Some banks restrict the amount of an overdraft which can be had at a preferential rate to a specific rate while others have no limit. All that they require is that the overdraft is agreed beforehand. If you borrow more than the specific sum, or exceed an agreed overdraft, the excess is charged at a higher rate. This is about double the preferential rate.

Borrowing by way of overdraft is generally the cheapest form of obtaining credit for students, providing you do not lose free banking. Since 1980, all lenders have been required by law to adopt a policy of truth in lending. The result was a yardstick whereby borrowers could compare the cost of one source of credit with another. Lenders must now calculate their interest and credit charges in a standard way. They key to the cost of credit is APR. What is APR? It is an abbreviation for the title 'Annual Percentage Rate of Charge for Credit'. To quote an Office of Fair Trading leaflet, 'The APR is a true cost of your credit – your clue to the cheapest way to borrow. Unlike most interest rates in the past, the APR includes all costs that go to make up the credit charge.'

Please note that APRS can never include the cost of operating a current account as bank charges vary according to how much the account is used. Also note that APRS (for running account credit – eg overdrafts) do not reflect any 'administration' or 'arrangement' fee for setting-up the overdraft. It is important to bear this in mind. Otherwise, it is true to say that the lower the APR the better the credit deal. Therefore, do not just look at the 'monthly' or 'annual' rates. An interest rate of 2.5 per cent per month may not look much, but it results in an APR of 34.5 per cent. APRS are always given greater prominence than any other rates in advertisements. If you consider it necessary you can always ask a lender for a Consumer Credit Act Quotation which will show the APR.

As always, in order to minimise interest charges, aim to pay back any indebtedness as soon as possible.

What to do if a grant cheque is late

If your grant cheque does not arrive at the beginning of term obviously it is financially inconvenient, but it is not a disastrous situation. Do not panic, but contact your LEA straight away. Quote the reference number from the letter you received advising that your application for an award had been successful. This will help to speed up their response. If you telephone, it is cheaper to do so after 1 pm and do not 'hang on' while the whereabouts of your grant cheque is being 'looked into'. Instead ask if it is possible for a person dealing with the matter to telephone you back with the response. Alternatively, arrange to telephone back at a specified time. Do not forget to ask for the person's name and extension number. All being well he or she will be able to advise you when your cheque is likely to arrive. Always check that your correct term address is on file. Contact your Student Union Welfare should there be any problems.

Your next step is to formulate an emergency budget to use until you receive your grant cheque. It would be prudent to add a week in case there is yet another delay. At the top of your list will be the cost of accommodation. If you are resident in hall, there should be no problem. Explain the situation to your bursar and ask if you may pay your rent when your grant has arrived. Such a request will be granted. Landlords in the private sector can also be understanding and there is certainly no harm in asking if you may postpone payment of your rent. Should he or she refuse, you could try to arrange to pay part of the sum due as opposed to the amount to cover the whole term. If you live in 'digs', your landlord may be a little uneasy about granting a newly arrived lodger board and lodging on account. However, he or she is only likely to want the money on a weekly basis.

The purchase of essential reference books and payment of society club dues can be postponed but daily living expenses such as food and travel cannot be avoided. Of course, it would be prudent to cut down on entertainment. If you are in self-catering accommodation, remember that many supermarket chains now accept Access and Visa cards. Nevertheless, the warning in Chapter 6 that 'credit cards can damage your wealth' should be heeded. If at all possible do pay off the whole amount owing by the 'due by' date.

Estimate the cost of all your expenditure which you will not be able to avoid. Be realistic and do not forget incidentals such as coffees and snacks, stationery and other essentials. Total your estimated expenditure.

Then total your resources – cash, bank and building society account balances. Deduct your budgeted expenditure for the period your grant cheque is likely to be delayed. If expenditure exceeds your resources then funds will be required.

Your parents may come to the rescue with temporary funds. If not, you will have to find credit from elsewhere. Borrowing from student friends is not recommended even if it is possible. The solution to your cashflow crisis is a temporary overdraft from your bank.

Overdrafts

All of the major banks have special overdraft terms for students. Some even lend up to a certain limit free of charge while others charge a preferential interest rate, which is generally 1 per cent over the bank's base rate on a portion if not all of the borrowing. This is a low margin and is well below the rate at which banks lend to personal customers. However, certain rules have to be followed.

An overdraft is made available for a certain period of time, for example a month or until the beginning of next term. Should the period prove inadequate, contact your bank before the end of the agreed period and ask for an extension.

It is absolutely essential that the overdraft is agreed with your branch.

The way in which you present your case for an overdraft is very important. Do not be tempted to overdraw your account before asking. Those who do so run the risk of not only losing 'free banking' (this could mean bank charges of £30 or more in a term) but will also not benefit from the low student interest rate. Banks tend to charge about double their concessionary rate for unauthorised overdrafts.

If you go overdrawn at the bank a letter may be sent asking you to 'rectify the position', or an attempt to cash a cheque may be referred by the cashier to a superior, thus making a quick call to the bank a lengthy visit as you are asked to explain why your account is in the red.

Ultimately you could suffer the embarrassment of having your cheques, which are not supported by a cheque card, 'bounced'. Incidentally when a bank does not pay a customer's cheque, a charge is usually made. This can be as high as £10 on *each* occasion. Certain banks also charge an 'administration fee' for an unauthorised overdraft and an additional sum when writing to customers about the state of their account. The fee can be as high as £10, indeed can the charge for a letter. It is therefore recommended that you play the banking game according to the bankers' rules, failure to do so could be very expensive.

Asking for an overdraft

Some individuals have a bout of nerves at the prospect of an interview with their bank manager. There is no logical explanation as to why a banker should be feared. Bank officials are merely business persons who assess financial propositions. Their aim is to lend profitably for the bank. As banks are anxious to retain their student customers after they graduate, they are generally sympathetic to reasonable requests. Also, they do not subject students to the same criteria as customers generally. However, in the past, banks have been criticised for making overdrafts too readily available to those attending university or college.

Consequently, do not anticipate muttering the word 'overdraft' to your student adviser, or other bank employee, and be given an unlimited authority to plunge into the red. Any borrowing must be justified. Also, do not forget that the sum you borrow has to be repaid at a future time.

When visiting your bank to discuss having an overdraft, it is best to make an appointment. Here are a few tips that will help you to make a good impression:

• State the precise amount of overdraft you require. It is wise to add a margin to allow for contingencies or for a further delay in receiving the monies which will regularise your account.

- Support your request with a copy of your budget. This will show that you have given the matter some thought.
- Give details of the source and expected time of the repayment. It would be useful, for example, to take with you the letter advising you of the amount of your grant.
- In order to reduce the interest charges, always pay available monies into your account immediately they are received.
- Should the amount of your overdraft later prove to be inadequate, or the period for which it has been granted prove to be not long enough, ask for an increase or an extension of time. Do not overdraw further or extend the period of your overdraft without consulting your bank. If an overdraft limit is exceeded you may lose your free banking and a higher interest rate may also be applied to the excess above the agreed overdraft.

If you do not bank locally

If you decide to maintain your account at a branch in your parents' home town, you could find that visiting your bank may not be convenient. If you followed our advice in Chapter 6 and arrange an 'in-case-of-need' overdraft before the start of term, no further action is required. Naturally, if the arranged overdraft is not sufficient for your needs, do not exceed it without asking. If an 'in-case-of-need' overdraft has not been arranged then contact your branch to request an overdraft. Follow the 'tips' given above.

When borrowing on overdraft, it is very important to watch out for the 'charge traps'. These can trip the unwary and can prove to be expensive. However, before examining 'charge traps' in detail, a free source of credit – credit cards – will first be outlined.

Credit cards

Not many people appreciate that a credit card such as Access or Visa is in fact two cards rolled into one. The cardholder can either use it as a charge card or as a line of credit. An American Express card is an example of the former. Each month the users of 'That will do nicely' piece of plastic must settle their account in full. Access and Visa cards can be used in this way too. As the time between paying for goods and services and settling the account in full can be as long as 56 days, it makes sound sense to use a credit card as a charge card. Although Access and Visa are accepted widely, plastic money is not accepted everywhere, so their use is only a partial solution to a cash flow crisis.

It may be considered tempting to repay only the minimum sum required by the credit card company. At the time of writing this is the greater of £5 or 5 per cent of the total amount outstanding on the account. The minimum payment is clearly given on a statement. However, this course of action is not recommended as credit card interest rates are about double the preferential rate students are charged on agreed overdrafts at banks. It therefore generally makes sound sense to repay the total amount outstanding, even if an overdraft has to be obtained.

As with all general advice there are, of course, exceptions. Mention has already been made of 'charge traps'. If one of these is spotted then it may be advisable to take advantage of borrowing from the credit card company. Although you will be paying a higher rate of interest, the total cost of borrowing may in fact be lower, if free banking is lost. As it can cost £30 or more a term to operate a current account students should try to avoid 'charge traps'.

In addition to paying for goods and services with a credit card, it is also possible to use them to obtain a cash advance. All that is required is to hand your card to a cashier at any bank displaying your credit card symbol and signing a cash advance voucher. If you have been issued with a PIN, an advance can also be obtained from an appropriate cash machine. This may appear to be an ideal solution to funding your out-of-pocket expenses. However, whereas there is a free period of credit when purchasing goods or services with a credit card, there is no such period when obtaining cash. Cash advances with credit cards attract interest charges from the day the cash is taken. As explained in Chapter 6, this may take the form of an initial handling charge (as in the case of Visa) or interest being levied on a daily basis (as with Access). The cost is roughly double the bank's preferential interest rate for student overdrafts. This form of finance is not generally recommended *unless* it is used to avoid a 'charge trap'.

Charge traps

Thankfully 'charge traps' are becoming more rare. All of the banks offer students free banking. However, this offer is subject to provisos. There are three basic criteria for free banking:

Case 1: The account is maintained in credit or within an *agreed unspecified* overdraft limit.

Case 2: The account is maintained in credit or within an agreed specific pre-defined overdraft limit, eg up £200.

Case 3: There are no stipulations as to the size of an overdraft or as to whether it is agreed.

You should be perfectly clear as to the criteria your bank has adopted before becoming overdrawn. Carefully read their students leaflet so you are absolutely certain of the conditions for free banking. Let us now examine each of the criteria in turn.

Case 1 You may not have the advantage of free banking if you stray over an agreed overdraft limit, eg become overdrawn by £101 when you have arranged a £100 overdraft. Careful management can avoid this situation.

Case 2 This is potentially the 'charge trap' situation. If you stray into the red without asking for an overdraft free banking may be lost. Careful management can avoid this situation. When you arrange an overdraft above £200, the trap will be automatically sprung and free banking will normally be lost.

Case 3 Last year three of the high street banks adopted this more relaxed approach. Regardless of how the account is conducted, whether it is in credit within an agreed overdraft limit or in the red without having first asked, banking will still be free.

If your bank has adopted the 'Case 3' criteria, you have no worries. Your potential danger is a 'Case 1' situation if your branch will not agree the overdraft you require. However, providing your request is reasonable and there has been no record of 'financial misconduct' in the past, you should not experience any problems.

Case 2 Situations can cause the biggest problems. There could be occasions when students with accounts at a bank adopting this criterion want an overdraft above the cut-off limit for free banking. For example, at the beginning of a term when a grant cheque has been delayed. However, all is not lost. You can ask at the time that the overdraft is requested, for all charges in operating your account to be waived. Should the request be refused, you can calmly advise the branch that you will have to contemplate moving your account to a bank with a more relaxed policy. This may reverse their original decision but should you meet an unbending attitude, it is still possible to avoid 'charge traps'.

Circumnavigating 'charge traps'

It does not require a great feat in financial manoeuvres to avoid 'charge traps'. To avoid such snares is not only financially worthwhile, but it also gives a sense of achievement of having 'beaten the system'. The key to achieving victory is your credit card. It is always astute to take advantage of the period of free credit. However, what happens when the day of settlement arrives and you do not have the funds to pay off the balance without losing free banking? Quite simply, only pay the minimum amount due. Admittedly you will incur interest charges but the total cost of taking the credit will generally be less than foregoing free banking. To minimise the interest paid, pay off what you can afford as soon as funds are available. There is no need to wait until your next settlement is received. Simply take your card and payment to any bank displaying your credit card. The cashier will make out the credit slip for you. Keep the counterfoils as receipt of your payment until the money is shown on your statement.

If you are short of cash, it makes sound sense to obtain a cash advance with your credit card rather than forego free banking. As previously explained, the two major credit card companies, Access and Visa differ in their methods of charging for cash advances. Access charges interest on a daily basis. Consequently, when you have funds to hand, you should pay what you can afford of an Access advance so as to minimise the interest payment.

Payments are first applied to the outstanding balance from a previous statement, then to cash advances taken since the last statement date and then to expenditure on goods and services. With Access it also makes sense to withdraw cash in stages rather than all at once, as this will help to reduce the interest charge.

Visa operates differently. It charges a flat handling fee as soon as the cash advance is taken. If you obtain £100 with the card and the fee is 1.5 per cent, you will have to pay back £101.50 by the 'due by date' if no further charges are to be incurred. Should you not clear all of the debt by that date, interest will be charged on a daily basis on the amount outstanding from the 'due by date'. It is therefore not worthwhile paying back a cash advance taken with Visa before the 'due by date'. Bear in mind that with Visa you have longer use of an advance for your flat fee if it is taken at the beginning rather than at the end of the accounting period. If you are not sure when the period begins and ends, look at your previous statements.

Graduation loans

All students think that the transition from a grant to a job with a good salary will mean financial freedom. It cannot be denied that the leap from a maintenance grant and parental contribution plus wages from vacation employment in the summer to a salary of several thousand pounds does have a hint of a 'rags to riches' story. However, the financial passage does not always run smoothly.

The majority of individuals will want and need a break after sitting finals. Indeed, it would be imprudent not to enjoy a period of relaxation. Possibly the final term will prove to be a greater strain on your resources than you expect. In a period of intense study there is not the time to 'shop around' for bargains in the food line. Perhaps a break away from your place of learning may be called for while revising. By the time term ends, you could be financially as well as mentally drained. And preparations for starting a career are not without cost. There will be clothes to buy, possibly a search for accommodation near to your place of employment. In brief, there will possibly be a sizeable expenditure required before your first salary cheque is received.

The financial institutions are well aware of these problems. Having retained the loyalty of their student customers during their period of study, they are anxious not to lose them afterwards. There is no doubting that banks' student packages are 'loss leaders'. Banks profit after their former student customers become established in a career. There is then the possibility of good business – personal loans, possibly a mortgage, perhaps an insurance policy or investment advice. As those who have undertaken a period of further education generally have a higher income than those who have not, it makes sound sense for banks to assist financially the new graduate or college leaver during this transitional period. This gesture of good will is, of course, in the hope of retaining their customer's business for life.

There is a growing tendency for the banks to continue free banking for graduate customers, who would otherwise not qualify, right up to the end of the calendar year after the completion of their course. Providing a qualification has been obtained and there is a firm offer of a job, a graduation loan on preferential terms may also be offered. It would be prudent, and indeed you may be advised, to transfer any overdraft to such a loan facility. 'Preferential terms' incidentally does not always mean at a preferential interest rate. Generally the banks allow the customer to postpone repayments of the advance for a few months until they are financially stable. If you do require funds after your course, it makes sense to take advantage of such an offer. It is also recommended that you transfer an overdraft to such a loan and maintain your current account in credit.

Special loans

Certain banks offer special schemes for medical and dental students. The packages vary from one financial institution to another, but generally they feature a preferential interest rate, no repayments at all during the period of study and postponement of repayments for a period after the course has finished. There are also similar loans for those who decide to attend law school after graduation. As all special loan schemes vary, it is wise to find the package that best suits your needs.

Asking parents for extra money could lead to friction and an inquest into lifestyle.

CHAPTER 9

The
First Term

'You cannot create experience,
you must undergo it.'

Albert Camus

THE BIG DAY arrives, you say goodbye to your family
and friends and embark upon a journey into the
unknown. What you have worked towards over the
years has now come to fruition. You have, more or less,
total independence and the next three years is yours to
make of as you wish – providing, of course, your
academic work does not fall below a certain standard.
There will be new friends, a different approach to
studying, a host of activities in which to participate and
a good social scene. With so many diversions it is
important not to forget why you are there – to gain an
academic qualification. It is important to combine your
studying and leisure activities in a balanced proportion
which is best suited for you as an individual. Your first
taste of further education is likely to be totally different
to anything else you have experienced. Rest assured,
you will not be alone. Indeed, all 'freshers', as the new
in-take is called, will be in the same situation. So as to
familiarise the new arrivals with their surroundings and
to make them feel 'at home', there is generally a
settling-in period known as 'freshers' week'. This chapter gives some advice regarding the financial implications of your first term.

Freshers' week

First year students arriving at an institution of higher education at the start of their first term may be forgiven for thinking that they are entering a social season. Rest assured, the serious work does begin after the initial round of introductions. You will meet your fellow students and the academic staff. There will be formal 'drinks', parties and informal gatherings. You will get to know the other students on your course and your neighbours in halls of residence or other accommodation. Friendships which could last a life time will be formed while some boon companions during freshers' week could be mere nodding acquaintances by mid-term. While doing the social rounds, do not get carried away financially. During our researches we encountered Richard, who parted with more money than he bargained for during the first couple of weeks of his first term. 'In my first term, I got through £300 in two weeks and I did not buy a single book! The problem is that first years have got a sizeable sum of money. It is probably the largest sum that they have ever had and they just watch it vanish.'

Richard's experience is by no means unique. Enjoy freshers' week by all means, but do not embark upon a course towards bankruptcy.

Freshers' fair

At this time banks, societies and clubs all set up their stalls to tempt you. The banks are there to compete for your accounts. However, as previously advised it is far better to have sorted out your banking arrangements at least three weeks before the term begins. There are far more interesting things to do at the start of term than completing formalities with a bank.

The range of extra activities you may be able to pursue during your course is diverse. There will generally be the usual sports facilities, with perhaps the opportunity for mountaineering, potholing or rambling. For the less energetic there may be croquet or bowls.

The arts are usually well catered for with the opportunity to join a drama society, film club, poetry society and photographic club, to name but four. The political parties will be represented as well as the various 'good causes' run by students – for example, a group which visits a local mental hospital, or does other work in the community. Also do not forget the academic clubs which will give you extra depth into your subject. Whether your interest is butterflies or debating, sporting activities or politics, there is bound to be something to suit you. Should your own interest not be catered for, there is always the possibility of a specialist society outside university/college. The local library will be able to advise. You could always think about starting a society yourself. Advertise in the campus newspaper to see if there is sufficient interest.

It is important not to join everything. There are two aspects to take into account – time and money. Both are scarce resources. While you may wish to pursue half a dozen interests, your academic work-load is as yet unknown and you may not be able to devote six evenings a week and every weekend to various activities. There is also the financial aspect, £5 here and £10 there may not seem much in isolation, but the total can mount up. In certain cases, a membership fee is only the beginning. Special clothing or equipment may have to be purchased for some activities. There is no point in spending money on items that you are not going to use. So, do not get carried away. Join the clubs and societies that really interest you and consider joining others later if time permits.

Books

There is no doubt that specialist academic books are expensive. Probably even before your departure from home, your department or faculty will send you a long book list. Do not panic, you are not expected to read everything, and you are also not required to purchase every tome mentioned. Indeed, to do so could well be beyond your resources. There will be certain text books which you will have to obtain. This will be stated either on the reading list or you will be advised at your first lecture. Before going on a mad spending spree, chat with those who have undertaken the course in the previous year. Rest assured, there is nothing more infuriating towards the end of term when funds are running low than to look at expensive books which have been un-opened since the beginning of term. Do not just rely on one person's views, but get a good consensus of opinion. Your tutor will also be pleased to advise.

If there are two alternative required purchases, go to the book shop and look at both. Perhaps the style of one appeals to you more than another. If the academic standard is the same, you are best to purchase the tome that you find easier to read. Many of the books which are on the reading list are there to give you greater depth into the subject as opposed to being an essential reference work. Naturally, if you have a particular interest in the area it covers, for example it is likely to be a 'special subject' of yours, it may be worthwhile buying it. However, proceed cautiously with book purchases initially. You will know which books you really want to own later in the course.

Sharing books

This route may appear to be an ideal solution. A friend purchases one particular volume and you another. You both have access to the books as and when required. Unfortunately idealism does not always work out in reality. There is an added complication at the start of a course in that you probably have not formulated any real friendships. Then there is the problem of who keeps what. It is likely that both of you will want the volume at the same time or if periods have been allocated under a shared arrangement, one of you has not finished with it when the other needs the work. There are better things to do than squabble over books. Enter shared arrangements with caution. As time progresses you may find an individual with whom you could share but until that time arrives, try to remain independent on the book front.

Buying secondhand books

It is not necessary to purchase new books as universities/colleges have secondhand bookshops run by students. Generally secondhand books sell for two-thirds of their current new price. If this facility is not available to you, check notice boards to see if a second year student wishes to dispose of volumes you want. Half to two-thirds of the new price would be reasonable. However, as long as you pay less than it would cost you new, you are on to a winner. If the tome is not in good condition, or is smothered with margin notes in ink, obviously adjust the price you are prepared to pay. It makes sound sense to take care of your own books, not only because books should be treated with respect, but for financial reasons. If these tomes are not required in your second year, you may be able to sell them on. This will relieve your financial situation the following year.

When buying secondhand books, do ensure that you purchase the very latest edition. A book in its second edition is naturally a revision of its first. It will be up-dated to take account of new research or ideas, etc. To use an old edition could well be detrimental to your studies. As an edition becomes 'out of date' it will also be worth considerably less than a secondhand copy of the current edition. If the revision is basically 'superficial', but with an additional chapter, then the purchase of the old edition *may* be worthwhile to give you the basics of the subject. However, refer to your department or faculty before purchasing the old edition. Additional material can always be found in a library copy.

Libraries

University/college libraries are generally useful sources for obtaining books. The authorities realise that certain volumes may want to be referred to by almost every individual on a course. Finances will not stretch to buying a copy for everyone, so a period of 'short' loan has been developed. 'Short' can mean a few hours or overnight. The period may appear very brief, but in a concentrated period of study and note-taking it is amazing how much can be absorbed in a few hours. Indeed, any longer period of loan would see decreasing returns for your effort. The human mind can only give absolute attention to a particular subject for a certain time span.

Most libraries have a reservation system for short loan books. Those of you who are able to fall out of bed at a reasonably early hour on a Saturday morning may be lucky to secure a tome for the weekend. Return all library books on time, not only to avoid being fined (the rate for 'short' loan category books is high), but also out of consideration for your fellow students.

If you are studying at an institution in a large city, municipal or other specialist libraries may stock certain books. Investigation can be well worthwhile.

Buying books new

Near most places of higher education, if not on the campus itself, there are usually bookshops to meet students' needs. Their owners liaise with various academic departments in the area and try to stock sufficient books to meet the needs of local students. Book distribution in this country is generally diabolical (ask any bookshop proprietor). If you cannot obtain an essential text book locally then either contact one of your school friends who is studying elsewhere or a bookshop such as Dillons in London, and see if you can beat the system with your own initiatives.

Bookshops which serve universities/colleges realise that students *have* to purchase books. It therefore may not be possible to pay for books other than by cash or cheque. However, if you do have a credit card, and these are accepted by the bookshop, it makes sense to utilise the facility and have the use of the funds until such time that your credit card company needs reimbursing. With this method of payment, you can obtain up to 56 days free credit. However, do not forget to record your credit card purchases when up-dating your own financial records to keep track of your expenditure.

Economies

'Look after the pennies and the pounds will look after themselves.' The only problem with this proverb is that it encourages people to be careful when saving pence and entirely ignore larger savings of pounds.

When resources are limited, it makes sound sense to look out for the 'best buys'. Some branches of the NUS issue their own guides to the locality. In addition to including a good pub and restaurant guide – which itself is invaluable – hints are given for shopping and entertainment generally. Local arrangements may have been made with shops, restaurants and cinemas which give discounts to students. There are, of course, nation-wide offers.

National Union of Students' Card: Discounts between 5 per cent and 10 per cent off a host of items ranging from notepaper to car equipment. Details are available from NUS Marketing, see Addresses of Useful Contacts.

International Students Identity Card (ISIC): This is obtainable from Students' Travel Offices or direct from NUS Services Limited (see Addresses of Useful Contacts) for £4.40. Proof of full-time education (eg NUS card, letter of acceptance to a course, etc), date of birth, nationality and photograph are required. Presentation of the card will result in discounts at selected hotels, restaurants and shops in London, Paris, Amsterdam, Brussels and throughout Spain, Portugal, Italy, Greece, USA and Canada. Vouchers are also provided for 'one-off' discounts, eg two 'Big Macs' for the price of one in Amsterdam. A *Countdown* card is also provided with an ISIC. This gives discounts at selected restaurants and shops in the UK as well as 'one-off' discounts at some stores and fast-food chains. There is also a pre-purchase voucher scheme which effectively gives discounts at British Home Stores, C & A and Currys. (Note, this information is based on the 1988 package. Check with

either your local Students' Travel Office or NUS Services
for details of the 1989 package).

Food

This section is for those of you who are in self-catering
accommodation as opposed to students living in a hall of
residence or other accommodation where all meals are
provided. A healthy balanced diet is essential. The
student who thought he had found the answer to the
rising cost of living with a diet comprising only of
porridge, discovered this was not a solution. He contracted something akin to scurvy. By 'economising on
food' it is not meant that you dramatically cut-back your
consumption, but that you eat food which is both
nutritious and offers good value for money. It also
makes sense to seek out the best buys.

It is not the purpose of this book to advise on what
constitutes a balanced diet. However, to economise by
skipping meals is no economy. Your body will lose its
natural immunity and you will become susceptible to
every infection that is doing the rounds. Not only will
your academic work suffer, but you will lose your income
from any term-time employment and will miss out on
the social scene.

If living on campus on a self-catering basis, you could
survive by eating in refectories. However, it is cheaper
to cook for yourself and even cheaper if several of you
club together. With a rota, it will not be a time-
consuming process. Naturally everyone will have to pull
their weight for this arrangement to work effectively.
Sensible shopping will also reduce your food bill. Here
are a few useful tips:

- Fruit and vegetables are cheaper at the greengrocers
  than in supermarkets.
- Meat is generally cheaper at the butchers than
  purchasing pre-packaged cuts in the supermarket.
- Supermarket 'own brands' are normally cheaper than
  well-known branded products.

- Keep a look-out for special offers and discount vouchers.
- Buying 'economy' or 'family' packs of items which do not deteriorate is cheaper than buying several small packages. Take your calculator along with you when you go shopping and work out which is the best buy.
- Only buy what you want. Make a list of your requirements and stick to it. Do not wander round a supermarket aimlessly popping every conceivable item that takes your fancy into your basket.

Clothing

Whether you are fashion conscious or just wear clothes out of decent necessity, it is possible to look 'right' and 'feel good' without spending a fortune. If you wish to be fashionably clad, it does not mean that you have to visit the trendiest boutique in town. A trip round the local market could well secure something very similar to the gear in a high street window at a fraction of the cost. It will not have a designer label or bear the mark of a well-known store. It could be a 'second' but the fault may be very hard to find. If you cannot bring yourself, for whatever reason, to shop 'downmarket' try to re-stock your wardrobe in the sales. If you keep an eye out for bargains, the odds are that you will be rewarded.

Oxfam shops and jumble sales can be another source of high-fashion, providing you choose the right decade. Some towns have 'nearly new' shops, which could yield just what you are looking for at a fraction of the cost. Do not look on purchasing secondhand clothes as acquiring someone else's cast-offs, but treat the exercise as an afternoon out. It can be fun if a group of you decide to see what fashion the local charity shop offers. As well as helping you out, you also know that you are contributing to a good cause.

Transport

Young Persons' Railcard and the *Student Coach Card* have already been discussed in Chapter 5. This section briefly covers two subjects – car ownership and 'hitching'

Students fortunate enough to have their own car are well aware of the running costs. There is nothing wrong in asking fellow students who travel with you to make a contribution towards your car expenses, for example, petrol. However, hiring your vehicle out for a reward, eg running a taxi service, will invalidate your insurance.

Finally, a word about hitching lifts. Campus sites generally have 'hitching-points' for lifts into town. Naturally a lift will save you the fare on public transport. You may be tempted to hitch further afield, but do take care at all times. Without wishing to appear condescending or sexist, women particularly should *never* hitch-hike alone.

Entertainment

Apart from a host of activities and societies that you can participate in, your local students union will organise events such as discos and concerts at prices which are cheaper than commercial events off-campus. The same applies to bars run by your union – prices will be far lower than elsewhere. The price of seeing a movie at the film club will also be a fraction of the cost of a ticket at the local cinema.

However, you may not wish for all your social activities to be centred around your university or college. Life on campus can become claustrophobic. As mentioned in the introduction to this chapter, some student unions publish guides to the locality which indicate good pubs and inexpensive places to eat. Discounts may be available on certain evenings if you present your NUS card or a local cinema may sell seats for weekday matinees at knock-down prices. Full details will be available from your union.

Christmas

The festive season can come as quite a shock. Even if you have been careful all term and managed to remain solvent, parties, dinners and discos which are organised can be an unexpected drain on your resources. No sooner have you finished the social round at university or college than you are back home meeting up with old school friends. Added to this there are gifts to purchase for the family. Christmas may be the season of comfort and joy but it is a strain on finances. You may find it useful to earmark some of your funds for the social activities occurring at this time of year.

Housing benefit

This subject is complex. Students, like anyone else, may qualify for housing benefit if they occupy accommodation as their home and they are liable for rent and rates, or a sum representing rates if an 'inclusive' rent is paid. Basically housing benefit is a weekly non-contributory benefit means-tested on both capital and income. It is proposed that students will not be able to claim this benefit from the start of the 1990-91 academic year (see Chapter 2).

Housing benefit cannot be claimed by students living in college accommodation, unless the college has entered into a 'head tenancy', ie it rents the property from a private landlord and sublets to students. Therefore those living in a hall of residence cannot claim housing benefit except during long vacations.

Those of you who are living in private rented accommodation should note the following from the *NUS Welfare Manual 1988-89:*

> *It is not always the whole of the rates or of what the claimant calls 'the rent' which is eligible for allowance or rebate. Some items in an inclusive rent may have to be taken out of the calculation altogether. Rent or rates may have to be divided between people including the claimant who are jointly liable for them. Income from tenants or sub-tenants may have to be deducted. There may be people within the household who are financially independent (non-dependants) and adjustments have to be made to account for their contribution to the household income. In addition, the local authority may*

decide that the rent in general is too high and may restrict the amount against which allowance or rebate will be paid.

It is worth noting that benefit cannot be claimed for poll tax, only rates. Poll tax is already in force in Scotland and will be introduced elsewhere in the UK in April 1990.

As a guide, students in April 1989 were entitled to claim housing benefit if their eligible rent was above that set out in Table 12.

TABLE 12
ELIGIBLE RENT STARTING POINTS FOR HOUSING BENEFIT

	£ per week
London	
Claimant 18-24	*24.93*
Claimant 25 or over	*20.06*
Elsewhere	
Claimant 18-24	*16.94*
Claimant 25 or over	*14.50*

1 On rent above the eligible rent starting point, housing benefit will rise with rents £1 for £1 up to the point where the rent becomes 'unreasonable'.

2 The examples above are for single, able-bodied and childless full-time students during their period of study. They assume no income other than a standard mandatory grant. The eligible rent starting points for the 1989-90 academic year will differ from the above; your local NUS will advise you of the situation at the start of the 1989-90 academic year.

If you qualify for housing benefit it is essential to submit any claim to your local authority as soon as accommodation is secured so as to ensure you receive all the benefits due. Care should be taken in completing the form. Refer to your college accommodation/welfare office if there are any points you are not sure about. Although local authorities are generally expected to make an assessment in two weeks, it can take several months for payment to be made. Sums above £2 per week can be paid fortnightly, while lesser weekly amounts are normally paid once a term.

Other state benefits

The general requirement that the claimant must be 'available for work' normally bars full-time students from claiming unemployment benefit or income support, except during the 'long' summer vacation.

Health care

Prescription charges
Students may qualify for exemption from prescription charges. Consult the DSS's explanatory leaflet P11. Application for exemption on low income grounds is made on DSS form AG1. Those who do not qualify but need several prescriptions would benefit by purchasing a 'pre-payment certificate' which gives unlimited prescriptions during its period of validity.

Dental and optical charges
In addition to the possibility of qualifying for exemption from these charges, students whose income is marginally above the limit for exemption can qualify for reduced rate treatment or services. The DSS issues explanatory forms D11 (dentistry) and G11 (glasses). Application on low income grounds are made on DSS form AG1.

In the case of glasses, the optician issues a voucher. If the patient is exempt from these charges he or she receives a full value voucher: a patient whose income is marginally too high for exemption may qualify for a voucher, the value of which is reduced by a contribution paid by the patient.

Insurance

Some insurance salesmen tend to descend on college campuses at the beginning of the academic year. They preach the virtues of 'providing for the future' and state, quite correctly, that younger people receive better life cover terms than those who are older. Our general advice is *not* to be persuaded to take out life cover as they will generally be offering whole-life, without-profits policies. While these are essential for married couples with children, so as to help provide financial stability when one partner dies, they are not appropriate for single people. Our advice is to leave such provisions until you can afford them. Then, always seek expert advice from either your bank, an independent financial adviser or from more than one insurance company.

If by chance you do have excess funds, do consider providing for your future. However, try to opt for a flexible arrangement. For example, initially the insurance policy may be slanted towards high life cover. Therefore you can take advantage of your age to obtain better cover terms. Ensure that at a later date there is the option to convert the policy more towards investment in the form of a lump sum return after a specific period of time. In other words, increased premiums are paid for life assurance. The policy could then be used for an endowment mortgage. However, only make such a commitment if you can really afford it, not only now, but also in the future.

The student who thought he had found the answer to the rising cost of living with a diet comprising only of porridge.

CHAPTER 10

Facing Problems

'Students loathe to admit they are in trouble. We call it the "street credibility to the point of absurdity syndrome".'

The Authors

EVERYONE WANTS to have 'street credibility' but it is not an end in itself. There are occasions in everyone's life when it has to be admitted that expert help is required. To ignore a problem in the hope that it will go away is absurd. What was a minor hiccup could turn – without help – into a major crisis. In many cases, problems that are tackled in their early stages can soon be put to rights. Moreover, when the odds appear, from a personal standpoint, to be stacked against you, there is a tendency to think that your situation is unique. In all probability this is not the case. This book is concerned with finance and financially related matters, but our advice applies to all problems – when things go wrong, seek expert guidance.

Financial problems

While it is hoped that you do not have a financial problem, if you do then face it head on – do not ignore it in the hope that it will go away. Perhaps you do not feel that you can discuss it with your parents, as perhaps a lecture on the Victorian values of thrift will not, in your opinion, resolve the situation. The obvious solution is to see your bankers. Contrary to popular opinion, banks can be very sympathetic, albeit firm, when dealing with financial matters that have gone wrong. But do not expect a student adviser or bank manager to wave a magic wand to make everything vanish: what they will give you is time to put matters to rights. Possibly a loan will be made available that can be repaid or reduced by earnings from vacation employment.

It is important to reveal everything to them regarding your finances. Many businessmen who have financial difficulties try to conceal the extent of their problems from their bankers. It all comes out into the open in the end, so 'come clean' from the start however embarrassed you may feel. Rest assured, it is far more embarrassing at a later date to return revealing another unresolved issue and requesting further help. That would be a real case of losing 'street credibility'.

Perhaps you would not feel comfortable going to your bankers. Despite efforts made by the banks to become more approachable, it is not always easy to pop along and admit to them that you are in a financial mess. We are reminded of a conversation we had with a bank manager responsible for a campus branch:

> *Yes, students are fiercely independent. They will go to their welfare officer, something we encourage them to do, but they only do it as a last resort. The general attitude is, 'I've come here and I'll manage.' If they are away from home they feel they are a fully mature adult and can cope with everything. There is no way they are going to admit to* anybody *that they are floundering. To actually go and say to someone, 'I'm in a financial mess', does not come easily.*

How true this statement is. But the fact is that if you do nothing, the situation will undoubtedly get worse rather than better. Most further educational establishments have a welfare office. You will find their staff welcoming, friendly and discreet. They have two main functions

– to provide information and guidance. Rest assured, confidentiality is strictly observed. With your permission they will liaise with your bank on your behalf. However, do bear in mind that welfare offices are not blessed with vast resources of staff, so what you can do for yourself under their guidance will ease the pressure on their organisation.

An alternative source of advice is your local Citizens Advice Bureau. Staff are trained to deal with all sorts of problems but, of course, unlike college welfare officers, they are not specifically trained to deal with student problems.

Financial problems are not always isolated cases of mis-managing money. While there may not be some underlying cause it is worthwhile sitting down and *honestly* asking yourself how you got into such a financial disarray. Some people spend money in order to cheer themselves up or because of a feeling of insecurity and a wish to become 'one of the crowd', or perhaps because of an addiction. If there is a possible reason, identify it and take appropriate action, or seek advice. However, you have to be honest with yourself. If you have just been financially irresponsible, you will have to put it down to experience and learn from the errors of your ways.

Accommodation problems

Accommodation problems are dealt with in Chapter 5 and briefly cover harassment and eviction. Housing is a complex field and there is no substitute for expert advice based on individual circumstances. If you face accommodation problems consult your local NUS, college welfare office or Citizens Advice Bureau immediately. Under no circumstances, except with the landlord's written agreement, stop paying your rent.

A message from the authors

We hope you have found *The Student Money Guide* useful and that it will prepare you for the non-academic side of university or college life. Our objective in writing this book was to provide a practical work which will smooth the way for those embarking on courses of further education. The project is a little like painting the Forth Bridge – it will never end. As soon as this volume is off the press we will begin our researches again.

In a constantly changing world certain problems vanish while others arise. We plan to up-date the *Guide* each year and introduce new topics as situations change. We keep closely in touch with students and student organisations throughout the year. However, if you feel there are subjects that should be included, or improvements which can be made, please do not hesitate to write to us at:

William Curtis Limited
83 Clerkenwell Road
London EC1R 5AR.

We wish you well in your studies and hope that the *Guide* will not only smooth your pathway to obtaining a qualification, but will also serve as a solid foundation for arranging your finances beyond your course.

Do not expect a student adviser or bank manager to wave a magic wand.

APPENDIX

The National Union of Students

England

Nelson Mandela House
461 Holloway Road
London N7 6LJ
01-272 8900

NUS Marketing
see above address

NUS Services Ltd
Rigby House, 4 The Parade
Watford WD1 1LN
0923-55300

Northern Ireland
11 Fitzwilliam Street, Belfast 7
0232-244641

Scotland
12 Dublin Street
Edinburgh EH1 3PP
031-556 6598

Wales
107 Walter Road, Swansea SA1
5QQ
0792-43323

Bank 'hotline' numbers

Barclays Bank plc
Barclaybank card or Barclaycard
0604-230230

Clydesdale Bank plc
041-331 1777

Access
041-552 1210

Other cards

The Co-operative Bank plc
Visa, Electron or cheque cards
0695-26621

Lloyds Bank Plc
Cashpoint cards
01-626 1500

Access cards
0702-362988

Visa cards
01-283 7302

Midland Bank plc
Autobank or AutoCheque cards
01-260 8000 or
0733 502995 or
0800-622101 (Note a Freefone line)

Access cards
0703-352211

National Westminster plc
Servicecards and cheque cards
01-588 3600

Access cards
0702-352255

Royal Bank of Scotland
Access cards
0702-351303

Cashline cards
031-556 7001 or 01-623 9000

*TSB England and Wales and TSB
Scotland*
Trustcard or SpeedBank cards
0273-204471

Miscellaneous addresses

The British Academy
Postgraduate Studentship Office
Block 1, Spur 15
Government Buildings
Honeypot Lane
Stanmore HA7 1AZ
01-951 5188

British Council
65 Davies Street
London W1Y 2AA
01-499 8011

*Central Council for Education and
Training in Social Work*
Student Grants Section
3rd Floor
261-265 Grays Inn Road
London WC1X 8QT
01-833 2524

*Department of Agriculture and
Fisheries*
Chesser House, Gorgie Road
Edinburgh EH11 3AW
031-443 4020

Appendix

Department of Education and
Science
Elizabeth House, York Road
London SE1 7PH
01-934 9000

Department of Education and
Science
Publications Despatch Centre
Honey Pot Lane, Canons Park
Stanmore HA7 1AZ
01-951 5188

Department of Health and Social
Security
Contact local office or Dial 100 and
ask for Freefone DHS

Economic and Social Research
Council
Research and Training
Administration Division
160 Great Portland Street
London W1N 6DT
01-637 1499

Education and Library Boards

Belfast
Howard House
1 Brunswick Street
Belfast BT2 7QA
0322-229211

South East
18 Windsor Avenue
Belfast BT9 6EF
0232-663641

North East
County Hall, 182 Galgorm Road
Ballymena Co. Antrim
BT42 1HN
0266-3333

South
3 Charlemont Place, The Mall
Armagh BT61 9AZ
0861-523811

West
1 Hospital Road
Omagh Co. Tyrone BT79 0AW
0662-449311

Endsleigh Insurance Services
Endsleigh House
Ambrose Street
Cheltenham GL50 3NR
0242-223300

Harrison Beaumont (Insurance
Brokers) Ltd
4 Meadow Court, High Street
Witney OX8 6LP
0993-3251

International Voluntary Service
53 Regent Road
Leicester LE1 6YL

Ministry of Agriculture, Fisheries
and Food
Room 116
Great Westminster House
London SW19 2AE
01-216 7406

Natural Environment Research
Council
University Support Section
Polaris House
North Star Avenue
Swindon SN2 1EU
0793-40101

Science and Engineering Research
Council
Postgraduate Training Support
Section
Polaris House
North Star Avenue
Swindon SN2 1EW
0793-2622

Scottish Education Department
Awards Branch
3 Redheughs Rigg
Edinburgh EH12 9HH
031-556 8400

University Central Council on
Admissions
PO Box 28
Cheltenham GL50 1HY
0242-222444

INDEX

Notes

Notes

Notes

Notes

Notes

Notes

Notes

Notes

Notes